BIRD'S-EYE VIEW

Keeping Wild Birds in Flight

ANN ERIKSSON

ORCA BOOK PUBLISHERS

Library and Archives Canada Cataloguing in Publication
Title: Bird's-eye view: keeping wild birds in flight / Ann Eriksson.
Names: Eriksson, Ann, 1956– author.
Description: Series statement: Orca wild | Includes bibliographical references and index.
Identifiers: Canadiana (print) 20190177489 | Canadiana (ebook) 20190177497 |
ISBN 9781459821538 (hardcover) | ISBN 9781459821545 (PDF) | ISBN 9781459821552 (EPUB)
Subjects: LCSH: Birds—Juvenile literature. | LCSH: Birds—Conservation—Juvenile literature. |
LCSH: Wildlife conservation—Juvenile literature.
Classification: LCC QL676.5 .E75 2020 | DDC j333.95/816—dc23

Library of Congress Control Number: 2019947370
Simultaneously published in Canada and the United States in 2020

Summary: Part of the nonfiction Orca Wild series for middle readers, this book looks at wild birds around
the world, the threats to their survival and what young people are doing to conserve their populations.

*Orca Book Publishers is committed to reducing the consumption of nonrenewable resources in the making
of our books. We make every effort to use materials that support a sustainable future.*

Orca Book Publishers gratefully acknowledges the support for its publishing programs provided by
the following agencies: the Government of Canada, the Canada Council for the Arts and the Province
of British Columbia through the BC Arts Council and the Book Publishing Tax Credit.

Front cover photo: Nigel_Wallace/Getty Images
Back cover photo: Bildagentur Zoonar Gmbh/Shutterstock.com

Edited by Sarah N. Harvey
Design by Dahlia Yuen
Author photo by Carol Sowerby

ORCA BOOK PUBLISHERS
orcabook.com

Printed and bound in South Korea.

23 22 21 20 • 4 3 2 1

Watching wild birds, such as this adult
female kestrel, connects you with a
fascinating and beautiful part of nature.
DAN SHAKAR/SHUTTERSTOCK.COM

*Dedicated to the Thetis Island Nature Conservancy
and bird lovers of all ages everywhere*

CONTENTS

Be gentle with nature. It's amazing—
and hard to get back once it's gone.
NANCY SALMON/GETTY IMAGES

INTRODUCTION

While visiting a friend on her family farm when I was eight, we found a soft, cup-shaped nest woven out of dry grasses and twigs in a tree near the barn. Three pale-blue eggs the size of my thumb were nestled in the bottom. "Robin," my friend whispered. I had never seen anything so beautiful. I reached in and picked one up. To my dismay it cracked in my hand, the yellow yolk spilling out over my fingers. I felt terrible, and in that instant I understood both the wonder and the fragility of nature. That encounter is my first memory involving a wild bird.

While I'm not an *ornithologist* (a scientist who studies birds), in my profession as a biologist and conservationist I sometimes work on projects that involve birds. I've come to appreciate them for their variety, their beautiful plumage and their fascinating behaviors. Most of all, I marvel at their ability to fly. People like me, who love wild birds, value them because they exist, like us, as part of nature. This is called *intrinsic value*. Wild birds also have value because they provide *ecosystem services*, which means they support and improve natural *ecosystems* and human lives. But many wild bird *species* are in trouble and heading for *extinction*. So take a bird's-eye view and learn why wild birds are important, why many are in trouble and what you can do to help. Maybe, if you're lucky, you'll also learn how to fly.

> If you listen to birds, every day will have a song in it.
>
> —Kyo Maclear, *Birds Art Life: A Year of Observation*

I love to be outdoors with birds and other wildlife every day.
GARY GEDDES

1

A gentoo penguin enjoys a walk on a beach in the Falkland Islands.
FIELDWORK/SHUTTERSTOCK.COM

1

AMAZING AVIANS

EVERYWHERE YOU LOOK

Wild birds live in every ecosystem in the world, even in the middle of the ocean, at the frigid poles and in the driest of deserts. They come in all shapes and sizes, from the flightless ostrich of Africa to the tiny bee hummingbird of Cuba. Birds are among the most observable of our wild neighbors. We see them soaring overhead, paddling across water, flitting through trees, pecking at the ground or our backyard bird feeders, singing from fence posts. Sometimes we hear only their rustles, tweets, chirps and *songs*—the birds themselves are hidden nearby.

Birds are a lot like humans. They communicate with their world using the same senses that we use: sight, hearing, smell, taste and touch. Most are diurnal like us, which means they are mostly awake during the day and asleep at night (well, maybe not like human teenagers and other night owls!). Birds live everywhere that people live and are

Bar-headed geese can fly over Mount Everest, the highest mountain in the world. LENSALOT/GETTY IMAGES

The flightless kiwi is endemic to New Zealand, which means it lives nowhere else on earth. JIRI PROCHAZKA/SHUTTERSTOCK.COM

commonly seen. They are often colorful and fun to watch. They are not a threat to us. For these reasons, it's easy to like them.

There are a lot of birds to like. So far scientists have identified over 10,000 species of birds in the world. The variety of life in all its forms is called *biodiversity*. Bird biodiversity contributes to the health and resilience of the world's ecosystems.

WHAT MAKES A BIRD A BIRD?

An animal is sitting on a branch in a tree near your home. How do you know it's a bird? "It has wings and can fly," you say. Most birds can fly, but some are flightless, like ostriches, penguins or the kiwis of New Zealand. Lots of other animals, such as insects and bats, fly too, so maybe the animal on the branch is a giant beetle, not a bird. If you told me you know it's a bird because it laid an egg, I might answer, "Possibly, but snakes and turtles and many invertebrates lay eggs too." Birds are warm-blooded and have two legs, characteristics shared with humans. But humans don't lay eggs and differ from birds in so many other ways.

Ostriches, which are native to Africa, are the world's largest living birds.
MANTAPHOTO/GETTY IMAGES

Some fossils of *Archaeopteryx lithographica* are particularly well preserved. The word *Archaeopteryx* means "old wing." GRAUY/GETTY IMAGES

"What about feathers?" you ask. Thumbs up! Birds are the only living animals with feathers. Feathers keep birds comfortable and dry and come in many colors and patterns to attract mates or protect against predators. If you've ever held a feather in your hand, you know what the term *light as a feather* means. Along with hollow bones that are fused to create an extra-strong but light skeleton, feathers are an *adaptation* that gives most birds the ability to fly.

ANCIENT ORIGINS

Feathers are also a clue to the earliest beginnings of birds. Feathers were around long before birds and bird flight. Fossils of *Archaeopteryx lithographica* tell us that this feathered dinosaur the size of a crow lived 150 million years ago. With no strong sternum (breastbone) to support flight muscles, it likely was a glider rather than a flier. The discovery of *Archaeopteryx* fossils in Germany in 1861 provided the first evidence to suggest that dinosaurs might be the ancestors of birds. Since then bird-like fossils even older than *Archaeopteryx* have been discovered. *Xiaotingia zhengi*, a meat-eating, feathered dinosaur the size of a chicken was alive five million years before *Archaeopteryx*. The earliest known ancestor

TWEETS FROM THE FLYWAY

Some species of birds are resident birds, which means they can find the food they need and keep their bodies at the right temperature in one location all year. But more than half of the bird species in the world need to migrate, which means they must spend their time in two different places to find what they need. Sometimes those places are close together, and sometimes they are far apart. To get to those faraway places, **migratory** birds often follow routes that are used by so many birds that they've come to be known as flyways. There are three main flyways: African–Eurasian, East Asian–Australasian and the Americas.

No one has ever seen a living *Archaeopteryx*, but one artist imagined them to look like this.
ELENARTS/GETTY IMAGES

of modern birds, *Archaeornithura meemannae,* a wading shorebird about 6 inches (15 centimeters) tall and pretty good at flying, hung out in shallow-water areas in what is now China about 130 million years ago.

Have you ever made a wish by breaking a turkey wishbone with a friend? That forked bone you broke is called a furcula. It anchors the flight muscles of birds to the sternum and strengthens their wings to allow flight. The furcula is another key clue to the connection between birds and dinosaurs. For a long time, scientists thought the furcula was found only in birds. But then paleontologists discovered them in dinosaur fossils, and not just those of flying dinosaurs. Even *Tyrannosaurus rex* had a furcula, likely used for support to help the two-legged meat eater carry its prey.

Some groups of modern birds are super old. We know from the age of their fossils that loons, cormorants, gulls and the New World vultures that live in North and South America have been on earth for a whopping 55.8 million

Archaeornithura meemannae currently holds the title of "oldest known ancestor of every bird alive today." ZONGDA ZHANG/CC BY 4.0

Loons have been around for tens of millions of years.
JIM CUMMING/SHUTTERSTOCK.COM

to 65.5 million years! Fossils from the group that includes wild turkeys and chickens date back 30 million years. Around the same time that loons appeared, between the extinction of dinosaurs and the appearance of large meat eating mammals, huge, flightless birds such as *Diatryma* filled the predator gap. *Diatryma* was 7 feet (2.25 meters) tall and had a stout hooked beak and powerful jaws. Like the velociraptors in the movie *Jurassic Park*, *Diatryma* stalked the northern hemisphere, hunting other animals until it disappeared like the dinosaurs. Thankfully, *Diatryma* and its relatives are no longer around. But since their early start as feathered reptiles, birds have evolved into a mind-boggling variety of types.

ORDERING AVES

A little songbird with a white stripe above its eye is walking headfirst down the Douglas-fir tree in my yard as I write this. What's its name? Scientists love names. In biology the naming of plants and animals is called *taxonomy*.

Some scientists thought *Diatryma*'s large beak might be for cracking nuts, as parrots do. Other scientists concluded that *Diatryma* was a meat eater.
ALEX CHURILOV/SHUTTERSTOCK.COM

The scientific name for the bald eagle is *Haliaeetus leucocephalus*, which means "white-headed sea eagle."
DAVEMANTEL/GETTY IMAGES

Every plant and animal has been given its own two-part (*binomial*) scientific name in the Latin language, kind of like the two names most people have. One name tells us who your relatives are, and the other name is your very own. The scientific name of the bird on the tree is *Sitta canadensis*. The first name, *Sitta*, is the bird's *genus* name. It tells us which larger group it belongs to. In this case, the larger group is the nuthatches. The second name, *canadensis*, is its very own species name. A scientific name sets one plant or animal apart from all the others. No other species on the planet has the scientific name *Sitta canadensis*.

Another bird living on the other side of the world in China and Korea has the scientific name *Sitta villosa*. Its name tells us that it's closely enough related to *Sitta canadensis* to be in the nuthatch genus *Sitta*. But the two have some different characteristics and can't breed with one another, so they are two different species.

Scientists love not only giving living things scientific names, but also sorting them into categories based on their common histories and characteristics. All plants are sorted into the kingdom Plantae. All animals are sorted into the kingdom Animalia. Animalia is subdivided into smaller groups on the basis of how the animals are related. The group that includes humans, birds and all other animals with a backbone is the subphylum Vertebrata (commonly known as the vertebrates), which is in the phylum Chordata.

Within the vertebrates, birds have their own category, or class, called Aves. It is divided into 28 orders and 170 to 253 families (depending on who you ask). For example, eagles, falcons and vultures are all in one order (Falconiformes),

BIRD TAXONOMY

Kingdom	–	Animalia
Phylum	–	Chordata
Class	–	Aves
Order	~	40
Family	~	245
Genus	~	2,313
Species	~	10,738

King Phillip Came Over For Good Soup is a helpful way to remember the most important taxonomic categories in biology: kingdom, phylum, class, order, family, genus, species.
IOC WORLD BIRD LIST 2019/WORLDBIRDNAMES.ORG

Birds form flocks for protection, for warmth, to raise their families, to find mates or food, or to take advantage of aerodynamics so they can fly farther during migration without a rest. ALLESSANDAR/SHUTTERSTOCK.COM

TWEETS FROM THE FLYWAY

Did you know that one name for a flock of crows is a murder? The names given to flocks of birds often relate to behavior or personality. Some make sense, like a drumming of woodpeckers, a happiness of larks, a pandemonium of parrots, a party of jays or a ballet of swans. I can't imagine where other terms come from, such as a banditry of chickadees, a kettle of hawks, a committee of vultures or a college of cardinals. The one that makes me laugh the most is a slurp of sapsuckers.

penguins in another (Sphenisciformes), parrots in a third order (Psittaciformes) and so on. The largest order is the perching birds (Passeriformes), which has 82 families and almost 6,000 species—more than half of the world's birds! Latin scientific names are not only fun to pronounce but also help us understand and recognize birds according to their common characteristics.

That compact little bird hopping down the tree with its strong feet and curved claws also has one or more *common names*. A common name is more casual than a scientific name. It can be given to a species by anyone, not just by scientists. I know the bird as the red-breasted nuthatch. Someone somewhere else might call it something different. Migratory birds might have a particular common name in one place and a different one in another. Many birds in North America were given the common names of similar-looking European birds. For example, robins in North America are not related at all to the European robin, but both have red coloration. The names used in this book are common names because they are easier for most people to remember. Learning the scientific and common names for the birds you see opens a whole new world of understanding. And it's a fun challenge too.

Woodpeckers are part of the family Picidae, which also includes sapsuckers, piculets and wrynecks. WANPHEN CHAWARUNG/SHUTTERSTOCK.COM

SUPER SIGHT

One summer day my husband and I were hanging out on our deck, enjoying the birdlife. A rufous hummingbird was eating at a nectar feeder just above our heads. We could hear the whirring of its wings as it hovered to feed. Suddenly a small falcon called a merlin shot over our heads, snatched the hummingbird out of the air, turned around and zoomed away. The whole hummingbird-napping took a split second. We were amazed at how fast the falcon could fly and turn and also at the winged hunter's ability to spot the tiny hummingbird from far away. It turns out that birds of prey, also called *raptors*, have the best vision of any bird. It's as much as four times sharper than a human's. Some raptors can spy moving prey from more than one mile (one and a half kilometers) away.

All birds see better than we do. They need to have excellent eyesight to fly quickly, evade predators and

Merlins eat mostly small birds. With sharp vision and powerful wings, these falcons attack their prey in midair at high speed. BILL PELL/DREAMSTIME.COM

The purpose of the barn owl's facial disk—the circle of feathers around its face—is to amplify sound by directing sound waves to its ears. HECK BENTLAGE/SHUTTERSTOCK.COM

capture prey that is fast-moving or camouflaged. Birds have larger eyes relative to their size than humans do. If our eyes were sized comparably, they would look like tennis balls in our eye sockets. Bird eyes are so large that they can't move around much in the eye socket. This means that birds can't swivel their eyes to look at something the way we do. Instead they move their heads. Owls, which can't move their eyes at all, can rotate their heads almost completely around. The eyes of a songbird are set wide apart or on the sides of its head. They can see predators (or you) sneaking up behind them.

When I look at a bird flying by my house, I might see a black bird with a brown head and tail. But another bird looking at that same bird flying by might see a turquoise body, a sage-green head and an orange tail. How do birds see so many more colors than humans do? All birds can see color. They have the same three types of color vision cells, called cones, in their eyes that we do. Each type absorbs a specific *wavelength* of light. Each wavelength

The eye-catching markings and extravagant plume on the head of this male California quail are bound to attract females.
KATYA KONDRATYUK

is translated by the brain into a color. The three types of cone in both bird and human eyes absorb the wavelengths for the colors red, blue and green. But birds have more of each type of cone in their eyes, which allows them to see the colors more clearly than we do. Birds also have a drop of colored oil in each cone that we don't have. This drop filters out more wavelengths and gives birds the ability to see more shades of color than we can see when looking at the same object. This allows birds to more easily see contrasts in their environment, such as camouflaged prey or other birds or, for diving birds, to see deeper into water.

Bird eyes also have a fourth type of cone that we don't have for seeing a wavelength of light called ultraviolet (UV) light. UV vision helps birds find partners and food. European kestrels and some other hawks and owls can track voles by following the UV trails created by their rodent prey's urine. Some berries and flowers reflect UV light, making them easier to find. The feathers of hummingbirds, American goldfinches and some other birds give off UV light, making them more visible to their potential mates.

Try looking in two directions at once. My weird brother can do it, but it's almost impossible for most people. It's easy for birds. Because of the way its nerves are wired, a bird can use its right and left eye for different tasks—say, one to find food and one to look out for danger. Birds can even sleep with one eye open, and some can even fly like that! Wouldn't it be fun to see through a bird's eyes for a day?

SENSING THE AVIAN WORLD

Hearing is the second most important sense for birds. Birds hear in a smaller high-to-low *frequency* range than we do but are better at recognizing different sounds. They also hear twice as fast as we do. When we listen to a bird, it's as if we hear only every second word. Imagine if your

Playing Bird Song Hero, a game in which you match a bird's song with its sonogram, can teach you to identify birds by listening. CORNELL LAB OF ORNITHOLOGY

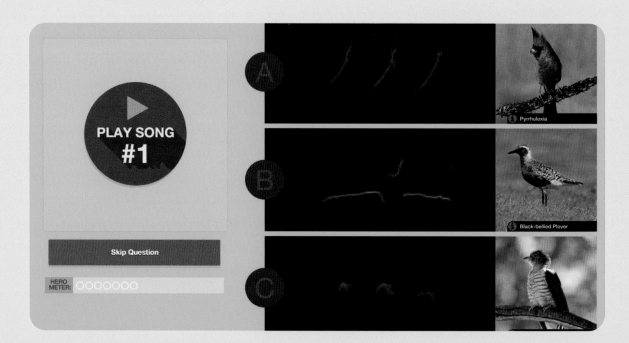

mom was saying, "No dinner, homework first" and all you heard was "No homework." By slowing down recordings of birdsong, we can hear what birds hear. Birds need sensitive hearing to detect the *calls*, songs or sounds of other birds and animals and figure out what they mean. Is the sound in the distance coming from a potential mate, a predator, another bird claiming territory or one offering to share food? Or is it food?

Bird ears are hard to see. They are located behind and below the eyes and are covered with soft protective feathers. Some birds have special characteristics that help them hear. Owls' faces have a round, concave collection of feathers called a facial disc that directs sound to the ears. One ear sits higher on the head than the other, so that the owl can better pinpoint sounds, such as a mouse scurrying under leaves. Some birds—like oilbirds, which live in caves—can echolocate like bats do, emitting rapid clicks and chirps that bounce off objects and echo back to them so they can find their way in the dark.

Birds also have a pretty good sense of touch. When birds fly, they need to feel changes in air temperature, air pressure and wind speed. Feathers, which don't have nerve endings themselves, transmit this information to nerves in the skin. Birds that feed on insects or drum into wood have special sensing feathers called rictal bristles around their eyes and their bills. Shorebirds and wading birds have specialized touch receptors on their long bills for feeding through mud and water. Have you ever wondered why penguins standing on ice don't seem to feel the cold? Bird feet and legs have few nerve endings.

A few birds, like kiwis, honeyguides, albatrosses, petrels, shearwaters and New World vultures have an excellent

TWEETS FROM THE FLYWAY

Modern birds don't have teeth, so the bill (or beak) is the body part they use for feeding, grooming and grasping. Some species of birds have small plain bills while others have large fantastical bills. The bills of all birds are designed to allow them to eat their preferred food.

The large bill of a toucan acts like an air conditioner, keeping the bird cool in hot tropical weather.
DAVID HAVEL/SHUTTERSTOCK.COM

If you had feet like a king penguin's, they wouldn't get cold when standing on ice. HTN/SHUTTERSTOCK.COM

sense of smell for finding food, but most birds have poor senses of smell and taste. Like humans, birds have an organ called the olfactory bulb that transmits smell information to the brain. The olfactory bulb in birds is thought to be too small to work very well. Migratory birds tend to have larger olfactory bulbs than nonmigratory birds do. The results of one experiment suggested that smell can be an important sense for helping some birds migrate. Cory's shearwaters fly long distances to breed on tiny islands in the Atlantic Ocean. When researchers washed the nostrils of a few of the shearwaters with zinc sulfate to temporarily neutralize their sense of smell, the birds couldn't find the way back to their islands. Imagine finding your way home in the dark using an odor map made up of the burger restaurant on the corner, the garbage can at the lane, the roses in your neighbor's yard and the aroma of your mother's cooking.

YOUNG BIRDERS

The American Birding Association (ABA) offers workshops, conferences, camps and conventions that bring young birders together to have fun learning about birds. ABA also hosts a Young Birder of the Year Contest. Adam Dhalla from British Columbia won the contest in 2018. Adam has been interested in nature photography, conservation and birds since he was seven years old. His photographs have appeared in various publications. In 2018 he was the youngest speaker ever at the International Ornithological Congress (IOC). You can see his beautiful bird photos at adamdhalla.com.

A.J. DHALLA

Arctic terns are sun seekers, migrating from the Arctic summer to the Antarctic summer every year.
KEITH WOOD/GETTY IMAGES

2

WINGED WONDERS

THE MYSTERY OF MIGRATION

The Arctic tern is a tiny seabird weighing only 3.5 ounces (100 grams), which is about as heavy as a deck of cards. At the end of the northern summer every year, these birds leave the Arctic and fly to the other end of the earth to spend the southern summer in the Antarctic. One Arctic tern tracked by scientists migrated an amazing 59,000 miles (95,000 kilometers). Why? Like people who go south every winter, Arctic terns are escaping the winter. They're also feeding on fish in both places. The Arctic tern's migration is the longest of any animal. In its 30-year life span, an Arctic tern travels the same distance as if it had gone to the moon and back three times!

Migratory birds navigate to and from places that are sometimes thousands of miles apart, frequently at night and through storms. First-year birds often migrate on their own, finding their way without

having ever traveled the route before. How do they do it? Migratory birds are thought to use a lot of different information to get where they are going. Sun, stars, magnetic fields, landscape features, wind, weather and even sounds and smells might contribute to a bird's "mind map."

How they might sense magnetic fields is still a mystery. One theory is that a special protein molecule in the eye might enable the bird to see magnetic fields as different wavelengths of light. New evidence suggests there could be magnetic sensors in the beak. Some scientists wonder if birds are hearing sounds we can't hear, with each location on earth having its own sound that the birds follow, as if they are "hearing the landscape."

The part of the brain that's responsible for memory and contains the mind maps animals use to navigate is called the hippocampus. A hummingbird can remember every flower it has sipped nectar from in a field of hundreds or even thousands of flowers. This allows hummingbirds to save energy by not visiting a flower twice. It turns out that hummingbirds have a hippocampus two to five times larger than that of other birds of a similar size and weight.

Birds aren't born with a map already installed in their hippocampus. They learn the map from their parents or from their environment, in the same way we learn from our parents or from experience. For example, young whooping cranes raised in captivity and then released have been taught by the humans who raised them to follow an ultralight aircraft to learn their natural migratory routes. Migratory birds know when to leave and how many days to fly in a certain direction. However they do it, migration by birds is amazing.

Male purple finches like this one
court females by hopping about and
fluffing up their feathers while singing,
often with a twig in their beak.
GLASS AND NATURE/SHUTTERSTOCK.COM

LOVE BIRDS

One of the species that comes to the feeder in my yard is the purple finch. Like many birds, the males of the species, with raspberry-red coloring on the head and breast, are more colorful than the females. In spring the male's color brightens. This tells me the finches are ready to mate, as some male birds, including the finch, attract females by their colorful feathers or other colorful or attractive body parts.

Other species perform elaborate courtship dances, songs or displays. Western grebe pairs dance a spectacular water ballet together when they are mating. Some courtships last for only a few minutes; others go on for days. Some birds mate with different partners every time, but 90 percent of all bird species bond for the mating season

The elaborate courtship display of western grebes is called "rushing." RYANSRUBINO/GETTY IMAGES

or even longer periods with a single mate, which is called *pair-bonding*. Some, like the wandering albatross or the peach-faced lovebird, mate for life. In bonded pairs, both parents share the job of caring for their chicks, a strategy that allows the pair to share the hard work of raising as many offspring as they can in order to carry on their *genes*.

No matter how birds find each other and mate, the result is one of nature's most perfect packages of nutrition and protection: the bird egg.

TWO IN THE NEST

A bird's egg contains everything the *embryo* inside needs to grow into a healthy chick. The yellow yolk is made up of energy-rich fats, proteins, vitamins, minerals and water. The egg white, or albumen, is full of water, proteins and disease-preventing *globulins* for the growing chick. The egg white also protects the embryo from heat, cold and impacts from outside. The shell, composed of a thin but hard layer of calcium carbonate crystals, protects the growing embryo from disease and bacteria. It has tiny pores that allow air and water to pass through. The shell is delicate enough that the chick will be able to peck its way out but strong enough to hold the weight of the parent during *incubation*, when the parent sits with its *brood patch* (a patch of featherless skin) against the egg to keep it warm. The egg shape is what gives the egg this strength. Try squeezing a chicken egg end to end between your hands. It's been said that an egg thrown the length of a football field won't break if it lands on its end.

Eggs come in many sizes and colors. All are laid by their mothers in a nest that was built by one or both parents. The nest protects the egg and hatchlings from predators

TWEETS FROM THE FLYWAY

If you find a baby bird out of its nest, check first to see if it is a nestling or a fledgling. Nestlings have no feathers and can't move very well. Fledglings have feathers and can hop or grip your finger. Carefully replace a nestling in its nest, if you can find it. Don't worry—it's a myth that the parents won't take it back. Fledglings usually don't need any help and won't stay in the nest if you return them. Their parents are usually close by. If you aren't sure what to do, contact a local wildlife rescue or rehabilitation center for advice.

Marsh warblers lay three to six eggs in a cup-shaped nest made of stems and leaves. Both parents feed the chicks.
VISHNEVSKIY VASILY/SHUTTERSTOCK.COM

and the weather until they are old enough to fly. Some nests are built on bare ground or are simple depressions in sand. Others are elaborate structures built with natural items such as grass, leaves, sticks, moss, branches, mud or hair. Odd artificial items like string, fishing line, plastic and broken glass can end up as nest materials too. Some waterbirds lay their eggs in floating nests. Hummingbird nests are delicate cups built out of plants and spiderweb. Some nests are used once. Others, like those of bald eagles, are added to every year and used for decades.

Some birds build solitary nests, while other species nest in colonies of dozens, thousands or even millions of nests. Guanay cormorant colonies can contain as many as four to five million birds. Colonies of sooty terns can have up to a million nests. That's a lot of birds! Social weavers in Africa build huge structures like apartment buildings, in which each female has her own nest chamber. The number of eggs laid in a nest varies widely between species. Most birds lay 1 egg a day. Wood ducks lay up to 15. You might find up to 50 eggs in an ostrich nest, but that's because many females share one nest.

DAWN CHORUS

Sit outside and close your eyes for 10 minutes. I can almost 100 percent guarantee that you'll hear a wild bird calling or singing. One scientist keeps track of house sparrows for research by listening for their calls or songs in the background of television or radio news from around the world. Whether in the middle of the city or in a rural area, birds are communicating with one another. Most bird sounds, called vocalizations, are produced by a special organ that only birds have, called a *syrinx*, located at the

The communal-nest "condominiums" built by social weavers provide shelter, food, homes and even a viewing or resting platform for other species of African wildlife. LIAM CHARLTON

During courtship flights, male snipes vibrate their tail feathers to produce a drumming sound that resembles the bleating of a goat.
NUWAT PHANSUWAN/SHUTTERSTOCK.COM

base of the windpipe. The syrinx has two thin layers of tissue, called membranes, that allow birds to create two sounds at once. As a result, birds can make some of the most complex and varied sounds in nature. How many notes can you sing in one second? Winter wrens can sing an incredible 36. Mockingbirds have seven sets of muscles and can produce 17 to 19 different songs a minute.

Vocalizations are used by both males and females. All birds produce calls, which are simple sounds for social interaction, like your friend calling hello to you from the other side of the street or yelling at you to watch out for that speeding car. Songs are more elaborate sounds that are used to attract mates or defend a territory. Some birds are born knowing their songs, and others learn them from their parents. Bird vocalizations are unique to each species, in the same way your signature or fingerprint is unique to you, so they can be used to identify birds by sound alone. Ornithologists record bird vocalizations outside and then recreate them in the form of a graph or visual printout of sound, called a *sonogram*.

Some birds also produce sounds by flying fast to vibrate their tail feathers (snipe), by inflating air sacs in their throats (prairie chickens), by hitting trees with their bills (woodpeckers) or by beating their wings to create a drumming sound (ruffed grouse).

MASTER MIMICKERS

As I waited outside a friend's house in Mexico once, I heard someone call, "I'm coming, I'm coming" when I knocked, but no one came. It turned out my friend's parrot was responding in her absence! Parrots, mynahs and cockatoos are champion mimickers. They can imitate

The male magnificent frigatebird attracts females with its large bright-red throat sac.
ADELIEPENGUIN/DREAMSTIME.COM

African gray parrots are so smart and such good talkers that some people call them the Einsteins of the parrot world.
INDEPENDENT BIRDS/SHUTTERSTOCK.COM

human speech—a huge challenge for an animal with no lips or tongue. A flock of wild cockatoos in the outback of Australia was heard swearing. Throckmorton, a pet African gray parrot, can imitate his owners' voices, sniffles, coughs and even their vomiting when they are sick, the sound they make when drinking water or coffee, their cell-phone ringtones and their dog's bark.

Other birds are excellent at copying sounds too. Some bowerbirds can imitate the roar of a chainsaw. The marsh warbler can produce the tunes of the more than 100 other bird species that share its habitat in Europe and Africa. Starlings, brown thrashers, nightingales and crows are also practiced imitators. A mockingbird in Boston once mimicked 39 bird songs, 50 bird calls, and the sounds of a frog and a cricket, one right after another.

THE TRUTH ABOUT THE BIRD BRAIN

Alex, a gray parrot living in a science laboratory, could count up to six. When asked how many red blocks were on the table, he'd answer correctly, even if he'd never seen them before. He could also recognize shapes, colors and materials, and he had a vocabulary of 100 words. Sometimes he got bored. The psychologist who worked with him said Alex showed the intelligence of a five-year-old child.

The biggest myth about birds is that they aren't very smart. A bird might look a bit dumb just sitting chirping on a branch or floating around a lake with its head underwater. Because birds have a smooth brain, not folded like a human brain, scientists thought birds acted according to patterns of behavior they were born with, called instincts, rather than intelligence. But it turns out there's more than

TWEETS FROM THE FLYWAY

I've been having fun using a free bird-identifcation app called Merlin, from the Cornell Lab of Ornithology, to learn the calls and songs of the birds that live near my home. It's hard to remember them all, but bird enthusiasts have created mnemonics—phrases that help them memorize bird vocalizations. Below are a few fun bird mnemonics. Maybe you can invent some of your own.

Olive-sided flycatcher:
Quick three beers

American robin:
Cheer-up, cheer-a-lee, cheer-ee-o

Willow flycatcher:
Fitz-bew

Song sparrow:
*Maids-maids, BUZZ,
put on your tea kettle-ettle-ettle*

Golden-crowned sparrow:
Oh, dear me, dear me

Mountain chickadee:
Cheeseburger

California quail:
McGregor

Barred owl:
*Who cooks for you,
who cooks for you all*

TWEETS FROM THE FLYWAY

Almost 200 years ago, finches in the Galapagos Islands helped English biologist Charles Darwin develop his theory of **evolution**. Darwin noticed that the beak size of seed-eating birds changed from one generation to the next on the basis of the size of seeds available for them to eat. During periods of drought, when there were fewer seeds, the finches ate up the small seeds. The birds that couldn't fit larger seeds in their beaks died. More finches in the next generation were born with larger beaks, an advantageous characteristic or adaptation inherited from their parents. When the rains came and there were lots of seeds of different sizes again, neither beak size had an advantage. The number of young born with small beaks returned to what it had been before the drought. Darwin called this process **natural selection**, whereby individuals with characteristics best suited to their environment would survive in greater numbers and produce young that also had those traits. He believed it was the way all life on earth had evolved. He wrote a book about his theory called *On the Origin of Species* that made him very famous. Evolution is thought to happen very slowly most of the time—for example, the transition from feathered dinosaur reptiles to modern birds took millions of years. But Darwin's finches showed that it could also happen quickly, even from one generation to the next.

Darwin's finches, from Charles Darwin's 1845 *Journal of researches into the natural history and geology of the countries visited during the voyage of HMS Beagle round the world, under the Command of Capt. Fitz Roy, RN*

one way to wire a smart brain. Scientists now know that birds have quite large brains—about 11 times larger than those of similar-sized reptiles. They know that bird brains are also packed with neurons, the cells in the brain that take information from the world outside and transmit it through the senses to the body, which then responds in some way.

There's lots of evidence for bird intelligence. Scientists and birders have watched birds learn and adapt to new situations, communicate well, remember and plan, solve problems and play. Some birds even use tools, a well-known sign of intelligence. A New Caledonian crow drops stones into a water pitcher to raise the water level so it can drink. The crow has learned how to change its environment to get what it wants. Green-backed herons lure fish with flowers, spiders and feathers. Yellow-crested cockatoos and African gray parrots use sticks to give themselves a back scratch. A crow and a jay were once observed having a "sword fight" with a twig. Woodpecker finches in the

Galapagos Islands use bits of the wood they've chipped from bark or cactus spines to reach into holes or crevices for grubs and beetles. These behaviors suggest that some birds are smarter than we often give them credit for.

AVIAN FUN AND GAMES

A man in New Zealand was driving down the road one day when a bird flew through his open window and stole a pouch of money from the dashboard. The bird was a kea, a parrot that lives in New Zealand. Known as "mountain monkeys," keas love to play practical jokes on unsuspecting humans. They play with objects and have been known to take apart tents, outdoor furniture and windshield wipers on cars, much to the annoyance of the owners of these things. Keas also love to wrestle with one another.

Not all birds play. Play has been observed only in mammals and in about 1 percent of birds, mainly those with larger brains and that care for their young for a longer time, like crows, ravens and parrots. While play is thought to be a way for young animals to learn and prepare for adult life, reduce stress and increase bonds with their parents, it can also produce pleasure.

Two ravens were once sighted sliding and rolling down a snowy hill. A crow was caught on film boarding down a roof on a jar lid; another, swooshing down a playground slide. Why else but for fun? Parrots are particularly playful and enjoy toys of all kinds. In laboratory experiments to study play in birds, no birds were observed to hog or fight over a toy, seemingly happy to share. Now that's clever!

New Zealand keas, known as "mountain monkeys," love to play with people's belongings.
TYPO-GRAPHICS/GETTY IMAGES

YOUNG BIRDERS

A re you interested in joining other young people to learn about birds and birding? Clubs for young birders can be found in many places around the world. Justina is a member of the Pasadena Audubon Society's Young Birders Club in the United States. She keeps excellent birding field notes. In 2019 she won a silver medal in the Field Notebook Module of the American Birding Association's Young Birder of the Year Contest (and a gold in the Writing Module!). You can join a club too. Check out the Young Birders sections at aba.org and ebird.org to find one near you.

There's lots of evidence that crows can recognize and remember individual human faces. Can you tell one crow from another?
FOREVERHAPPY/SHUTTERSTOCK.COM

3

ZOOMING IN ON WILD BIRDS

THE WAY TO A BIRD'S HEART

When eight-year-old Gabi accidentally dropped her snack in her Seattle yard, she didn't know it would make her some bird friends. A crow flew down and ate it. A few days later Gabi dropped more food, and again a crow ate it. Crows started to hang around near her house to watch for her. Gabi started to leave food out on purpose for the crows. She asked her mom to help her put up a bird feeder, which she filled with peanuts. To her delight, the crows ate the peanuts and in exchange left her little gifts like buttons, rocks, beach glass, a paper clip, a Lego piece and—her favorite— a pearl-colored heart trinket. Gabi and her mom are now enthusiastic bird-watchers.

Wild birds can be hard to see in their natural habitat. They hide in trees and shrubs, fly too fast for us to observe them easily or move

A homemade bird feeder can be as simple as a heart-shaped mix of seeds and suet hung on a branch.
INTHERAYOFLIGHT/SHUTTERSTOCK.COM

away when we get close. But birds, like us, need food every day. For a bird, finding food can be hard work that takes up a lot of time and energy. One of the best ways to get close to birds is to attract them to us by offering them the food they like, the way Gabi did with the crows.

Putting up a bird feeder allows you to view birds and their behaviors. Watching the birds at the feeders in our yard gives my family many hours of pleasure. One day I counted 15 species of birds at our feeder in just 30 minutes. My family is not alone. Throughout North America, 50 million bird lovers feed birds one million tons of seeds every year. That's a mountain of seed! But feeding birds doesn't need to be complicated or expensive.

It's easy to start attracting birds to your home or school with simple homemade feeders. Seeds, nuts and fruit appeal to a wide variety of birds. Be creative. Put a tray of sunflower seeds, peanuts or dried fruit outside on a table or railing. Thread some fruit chunks on a circle of wire and hang it from a branch. Reuse a plastic drink bottle to make a seed feeder with a pair of chopsticks or twigs for perches. Many birds like a mixture of animal fat (called suet) and seeds or fruit, which gives them quick energy in cold weather. Ask an adult to show you how to drill some holes in a short log. Next, fill the holes with a suet mixture or a combination of peanut butter and corn meal and then add a hook and hang the log outside. Smear peanut butter in the gaps of a pine cone, roll it in seeds and hang it from a string. Hummingbirds and other nectar feeders like a sweet mix of one part sugar to four parts water (no food coloring, please). Even a clean baby-food jar can become a hummingbird feeder. Check online sites like thespruce.com for ideas and instructions for making homemade feeders.

You can attract different kinds of birds by placing your feeders at different levels. Table-like feeders will attract ground-feeding birds such as sparrows, juncos and towhees. Hopper or tube feeders are good for shrub-and tree-feeders like finches and cardinals, and suet feeders high off the ground are good for treetop feeders like woodpeckers, nuthatches and chickadees. Leave out water in a shallow dish or bird bath for them to drink from and bathe in too.

It might take a few days for the birds near your home or school to find the food you leave for them. But once they do, they'll visit often. Once you start feeding birds,

TWEETS FROM THE FLYWAY

Did you know that hats and birds sparked the beginning of the conservation movement? In 1896 Harriet Hemenway and Minna B. Hall invited Boston society ladies to tea, where they asked them to stop wearing hats decorated with bird feathers. The efforts of these women and others who loved birds eventually led to the founding of the National Audubon Society in 1905. The organization, named in honor of ornithologist and painter John James Audubon, protects birds and bird habitat in the United States to this day.

Simple bird feeders are easy and fun to make and can be a good way to reuse containers. PAVEL L PHOTO AND VIDEO/SHUTTERSTOCK.COM

don't forget to keep filling up your feeders, especially in winter, when there are few other sources of food. The birds will depend on you.

TO FEED OR NOT TO FEED

Feeding birds is fun and interesting for us, but is it good for them? It's an important question. After all, bird feeders can spread disease, attract birds to windows and lure predators like hawks and cats. Scientists at the Cornell Lab of Ornithology decided to find out the answer to this question by studying information about birds that had been collected over many decades. They found that birds who visit feeders often are doing well. Their populations are growing, and they are living in more places.

So go ahead and keep your family's or school's backyard feeders full. But it's important to take precautions so you aren't doing more harm than good. Whether you're using homemade or store-bought feeders, follow these safety practices for feeding your avian friends:

- Keep feeders and bird baths clean to prevent yeasts, molds and bacteria from growing in them and to get rid of viruses and bacteria left on the outside by infected birds. Every couple of weeks give your seed feeders a good scrub with soap and hot water and then sanitize them by soaking them in a mild bleach solution (no more than 1 part bleach to 10 parts water) or full-strength vinegar. If using vinegar, soak for an hour. Rinse well with water and dry before filling. Regularly clean up seeds spilled under the feeder so they don't become a gooey mess that could make birds sick.
- Clean hummingbird feeders with very hot water every two to five days or whenever you see cloudy water or black mold.
- Remove your feeders for a while if you notice that cats, hawks, snakes, raccoons or other predators are around.
- Keep feeders out of sight of windows or place them within two feet (50 centimeters) of window glass so that birds must slow down to land and won't crash into the glass.
- When buying commercial birdseed, be sure it is not made with such fillers as milo, wheat and oats, which will go to waste on the ground. Look for mixes containing sunflower seeds, millet and cracked corn—the three most popular types of birdseed. They might be more expensive, but the birds will thank you.
- Use suet only in winter. Suet can turn rancid in hot weather, and the dripping fat can damage the natural waterproofing on bird feathers. As an alternative in

Filling my bird feeders and keeping them clean is a regular part of my day.
GARY GEDDES

summer or for use anytime, mix one part peanut butter with five parts corn meal.

- Store seed in secure metal containers with lids to protect it from rats and mice. Keep it cool and dry to prevent the growth of mold, and don't store it longer than one season.

ONE BIRD, TWO BIRDS, THREE BIRDS, FOUR

Once you have a bird feeder, birdbath or even garden plants that birds love, you have everything you need to participate in Project FeederWatch. Every winter from November to April, more than 20,000 North Americans count the birds that visit their yards and send the information to feederwatch.org. The information helps scientists track the movements of winter birds so they can figure out over time where the birds are living and how many there are.

Or join in the Great Backyard Bird Count (GBBC). Over four days every February, hundreds of thousands of people around the world count wild birds in their backyards and post their observations online in near-real time. They share photos and videos too. The GBBC gives an annual global snapshot of where birds are and in what numbers. All you need is access to a computer, a pen and paper, a bird identification book for your area and a place to watch birds. Sign up at gbbc.birdcount.org and, over the four days chosen for the event, write down the kind and number of birds you see in a 15-minute (or longer) period. Then share your data on the website. Participating is free and fun. In 2019 more than 200,000 lists of birds were shared, from 100 different countries. More than

2019 Great Backyard Bird Count

Count for the Birds!

The Great Horned Owl Award

This certificate is presented to

_____

In recognition of your great work counting birds
for the 2019 Great Backyard Bird Count!

David Bonter

David Bonter, Director of Citizen Science
Cornell Lab of Ornithology

Gary M. Lay

Gary Langham, Vice President and Chief
Scientist, National Audubon Society

Jon McCrac

Jon McCracken, Director, National Programs
Bird Studies Canada

The**Cornell**Lab of Ornithology   Audubon   BIRD STUDIES ÉTUDES D'OISEAUX CANADA   Sponsored by *Wild Birds Unlimited*

Participate in the Great Backyard Bird Count and you'll receive this great certificate. CORNELL LAB OF ORNITHOLOGY

6,600 species were observed. You can even enter your photos in the GBBC photo contest.

BUILDING FOR BIRDS

Another great way to attract birds to your home or school is to provide them with a place to nest. Building a nest box for a native bird species that might need one can be a fun project to do with your family or your school class. Different species of birds have different needs, so it's important to build your birdhouse with a particular type of bird in mind. You want your birdhouse to keep the birds dry and not too hot or too cold. You want it to

have the right size of entrance hole for the bird you want to attract. You want it to be easy for both adults and babies to get in and out of. It's important that it's designed to keep predators like raccoons, cats, snakes and chipmunks out. Build it so that it's easy to put up and clean regularly. You can download nest-box plans for safe birdhouses for different species from nestwatch.org. Once your birdhouse is up and occupied, you can sign up at nestwatch.org to become a certified NestWatcher. Send in your observations and join thousands of other NestWatchers helping scientists understand and study birds. You'll benefit by learning about birds and the natural world you share with them.

COUNTING FOR CONSERVATION

You can use your knowledge of birds to make meaningful contributions to science. *Citizen scientists* are volunteers like you and me who help scientists collect information they otherwise wouldn't have the time or resources to collect on their own. Some citizen scientists travel long distances to volunteer, and others do it in their own community. Many participate online without leaving the comfort of home.

The Great Backyard Bird Count, Project FeederWatch and NestWatch are examples of citizen-science projects that focus on birds. In fact, birds inspired some of the very first citizen-science projects. The Christmas Bird Count was started in 1900 by conservationist Frank M. Chapman, who suggested that hunters count birds during the holidays instead of shooting them. That year 27 people tallied about 90 species of birds from the 25 communities in Canada and the United States that held counts. Now tens of thousands of volunteers participate in the Christmas Bird Count (CBC) by counting birds in their own communities. It's easy to join in. Sign up on the Audubon Society website (audubon.com) in November and then go out between December 14 and January 5 with your family or friends or with an organized CBC group near you. It's simple. Make a list of all the birds

TWEETS FROM THE FLYWAY

You can help birds build their nests by leaving a bit of their favorite building materials at the edge of your yard or in a tree or bush. Cotton batting, dried moss, strips of bark from dead trees, short pieces of soft string or yarn, dead grass, small twigs and fluffy feathers are all good nesting materials. Then keep an eye out to see which birds discover your treasures and where they take them. You might be lucky enough to witness them building their nest.

Young Birder Sierra Glassman, from California, knows that urban birding can be as fun and interesting as birding in the wild.
STEVE GLASSMAN

Citizen science is even more enjoyable
when you share it with friends.
LESLIE BOL/NATUREKIDS BC

you see, how many and where you see them, and then go back to the website to input your data.

Another pioneering citizen-science program, the Breeding Bird Survey, uses volunteers to count birds along assigned routes during the peak of the breeding season. Today the Breeding Bird Survey covers more than 3,700 routes in the United States and Canada, and 3,200-plus routes in the United Kingdom, and involves thousands of volunteers. These programs and others like it help identify problems birds might be having. Recognizing a problem is the first step in solving it.

How easy is it to count birds? Have patience, get outside, and watch and listen, and you should see and hear lots of them. Nobody could possibly count them all, but scientists estimate there are between 200 billion and 400 billion individual birds in the world. Some are more common than others.

CATCH THE BIRDING BUG

Once your feeders and nest boxes start to attract birds, you'll begin to recognize the different species and learn about their habits and behaviors. You might want to venture farther from home to learn more about the wild birds that don't come to your yard. It's easy at any age to start watching birds. You can learn a lot about birds by simply using your eyes and ears to pay attention when you are in bird habitat. One way to start is by sitting quietly outside. Watch and listen. In a journal, write or draw what you see and hear to help you remember. Size and color are easy ways to tell different species apart. Where do they spend most of their time? On the ground, hiding among leaves, sitting in dead trees, swimming or flying? Are they

TWEETS FROM THE FLYWAY

The largest biodiversity citizen-science project in the world is for the birds. Every year an incredible 100 million or more bird sightings are recorded on eBird. Managed by the Cornell Lab of Ornithology, eBird is successful because of the cooperative efforts of hundreds of partner organizations, thousands of experts and hundreds of thousands of users. You can be an eBirder too. Just sign up at ebird.org and start sending in your sightings, photos and recordings so they can be shared with others in your area or around the world. And check out eBird's web page for everything a young birder needs to know about a life with birds.

People around the world take their appreciation of birds very seriously. Millions of people spend tens of billions of dollars every year watching birds. Bird-watchers travel the world to catch even a fleeting glimpse of a rare bird so they can put it on their Life List—a list of all the birds they have seen in their life. One British birder checked off a whopping 9,000 species before he retired at the age of 81. Another birder, Noah Stryker, sighted a record 6,042 bird species in one year! Bird-watchers buy binoculars, guidebooks, spotting scopes, cameras and recording equipment, airline flights, computer apps, ship passage, hotel rooms, meals, clothing and the services of guides. Add in the amount of money spent on backyard bird feeders and birdseed by other bird lovers, and you can see that avitourism (tourism that focuses on birding opportunities) and other bird-related businesses give a big boost to the economy of many countries and communities. If done carefully to minimize the impact on the environment, and with a portion of the profits directed to protecting species and their habitats, bird-watching can be good for both birds and people.

alone most of the time or in groups? How do they hold their tails? Do they have fancy crests? How do they walk? Once you start looking, you'll be surprised how fast you learn to tell one bird from another.

Borrow a bird-identification guide from your library and see if you can identify the birds you're seeing. Join other people interested in birds, and you'll learn from one another. You'll make some friends and have fun outdoors too. Birding is something you can do anytime and anywhere. Pretty soon you might discover you can't wait for your next chance to watch birds.

Around the world, young people like you are catching the birding bug. They are bird-watching, teaching classes, leading birding trips, volunteering at birding centers, conducting bird counts, banding birds, collecting data for ornithologists and advocating for better laws to protect birds and bird habitat.

MIND YOUR BIRDING MANNERS

I'm sure you've been taught good manners by the adults in your life. Well, there are good manners for bird-watching too. They help you and other bird-watchers have a good experience without harming birds or bothering other people. Remember that birds see and hear really well. Move quietly, like a ninja, and wear dark clothing so you won't disturb them. You'll see and hear more too. Prevent damage to bird habitat by staying on roads, trails and paths

TWEETS FROM THE FLYWAY

Once you start watching birds, you'll probably want a pair of binoculars to help you see them up close and track their movements. You might find a good pair secondhand, or you could ask your family to chip in for a birthday gift you'll use for the rest of your life. There are lots of things to consider when choosing binoculars for birding. All binoculars have numbers that tell you the magnifying power and the diameter of the lens. For example, a binocular labeled 7x35 has a magnifying power of 7 and the front lens is 35 millimeters in diameter. Most birders use 7x35 to 10x50 binoculars—8x40 is ideal. Look through many binoculars and compare them side by side. Select the binoculars that feel the most comfortable for your eyes. Wide-angle binoculars will help you locate and track birds. You'll be using them a lot outside, so you'll want them to be sealed and waterproof.

wherever possible, and always walk carefully through the environment. Respect the law and the rights of others. Ask for permission if you want to go on private property. Follow the rules in public places like parks. Be polite and courteous when you meet other people. Your exemplary behavior will generate goodwill with birders and non-birders alike—and with birds too!

MORE THAN JUST A PRETTY PICTURE

It's fun and interesting to learn about the wild birds we share the planet with. Knowledge about birds and bird life fills thousands of books, magazines and websites, and it continues to grow as we find out more about our avian friends. Ornithologists are still exploring the world and discovering new species of birds. The Sulawesi streaked flycatcher was discovered in 2014 in patches of forest left by farmers on that Indonesian island. In 2015 the Sichuan bush warbler was found living in the brush and in tea plantations in the mountains of central China. The blue-throated hillstar was discovered in Ecuador in 2018. To learn more about fascinating bird adaptations, biology and behaviors, check out some of the reading selections listed in the Resources section at the back of this book, go online, or browse your local library or bookstore.

The Sichuan bush warbler from China is one of the world's newest bird discoveries. PAUL J LEADER

YOUNG BIRDERS

Spending time in nature, and photographing birds like this snowy plover, helps Max Laubstein stay positive in a sometimes stressful world. He wishes people of all ages and backgrounds could experience the beauty of birds the way he does. Max intends to study biology in university. He's a member of the California Young Birders Club, which brings together birders aged 12 to 20 in chapters throughout California to have fun learning about birds. The club organizes lots of great field trips.

JONAH M. BENNINGFIELD

In Canada, birds that eat flying insects, such as the barn swallows that nest above my deck, are dropping in population faster than any other group of birds.
VIESTURS JUGS/SHUTTERSTOCK.COM

4

WHY WILD BIRDS MATTER

IN THE NEIGHBORHOOD

For the past few summers a pair of barn swallows has built a nest on a beam above the deck of my house. What a mess they make! When the eggs hatch, my husband, Gary, and I stop eating at our outdoor table because we don't want to scare the parents away from their chicks. But we are happy to have the little family because barn swallows eat a lot of pesky flies and wasps. Much of what birds do is not visible or audible to us. While they're flying, paddling, flitting, pecking, tweeting, chirping and singing, birds are also performing important ecosystem services that help keep nature (and us!) healthy and functioning properly.

SPECIAL DELIVERY

I'm always trying to take photographs of birds in my yard, but I'm rarely successful because they are rarely still. Birds spend their days on the move to find shelter, food or mates. As birds fly from place to place during their daily routines or during migration, they spread seeds, plants and *nutrients* near and far. In some tropical forests, birds are responsible for spreading the seeds of almost all (92 percent) of the trees and shrubs. More than 4,000 bird species are known to eat fruit. As they fly, they drop poop containing fruit seeds. The seeds of almost 69,000 plants (25 percent of all seed-plant species) are spread by fruit-eating birds in all ecosystems on earth except those covered by ice. Some trees, like African mahogany, rely on only a few species of birds to be able to reproduce. Without birds, some plants would disappear from the planet forever.

Some birds transport nutrients between different ecosystems, from ocean to land or from cities to forests.

The gallito de las rocas, a tropical bird of South America and the national bird of Peru, helps spread the seeds of the fruit it likes to eat. STEPHANIE STARR/DREAMSTIME.COM

Great cormorants in Izu, Japan, are excellent at transporting nutrients between the ocean and the land. YUZU/SHUTTERSTOCK.COM

For example, great cormorants in Japan live in both salt-and freshwater ecosystems. They bring large amounts of the nitrogen and phosphorus that's in their ocean food into the forest near the lakes where they nest. In Mexico, nutrients in grain transported by snow geese from fields to ponds help feed the fish and crayfish living there. Crows move nutrients from the city to the forests in their droppings.

Have you ever watched a robin scratch around on the ground for worms? When birds forage for food on the ground in forests, wetlands, grasslands and fields, they stir up the surface and tear leaves and other plant material into small pieces so that nutrients such as nitrogen are more easily mixed into the soil, ready to be used for growing more plants. Other birds dig to make nests or to feed. Burrowing owls nest in holes in the ground, parrots feed on soil, and some swallows nest on cliff faces or riverbanks. These birds are mixing the sediments, an important biological process called *bioturbation* (how's that for a good word for your vocabulary?) that helps recycle nutrients. Ecosystems with healthy populations of birds have been shown to have higher *primary productivity* (plant growth) than those where birds have disappeared.

Robins are doing more than eating their favorite food when they dig earthworms from the ground. LEA SPENCE/SHUTTERSTOCK.COM

Pollen grains stick to the head and neck of this little spiderhunter in southeast Asia as it uses its long, curved bill to suck nectar from the flower of the false-bird-of-paradise plant. NOICHERRYBEANS/SHUTTERSTOCK.COM

POLLINATION FOR THE NATION

A ruby-throated hummingbird in Georgia drinks sweet, sugary nectar with its long thin bill from deep down in a scarlet bee-balm flower. As it sips, pollen grains from the male part of the flower dust the hummingbird's head and back feathers. The hummingbird finishes drinking and flies to another bee balm. When it sips nectar there, it leaves some of the pollen grains on the female part of that flower. A seed is produced, which eventually grows into another plant. This transfer of pollen is called *pollination*. It's the way that most plants reproduce. Pollination by birds is called ornithophily. Another great word to know.

The wind, bees and other insects are nature's main pollinators, but more than 2,000 species of birds get in on the act. Hummingbirds, spiderhunters, sunbirds, honeycreepers and honeyeaters are all pollinators, particularly of wildflowers. These birds are attracted mainly to bright red, orange or yellow flowers with little scent and lots of nectar.

Many plant species would die out if they aren't pollinated. One-third of Hawaii's *endemic* birds (those found nowhere else) have been wiped out by human activity since Europeans settled in the islands. As a result, 31 species of bellflower plants have also become extinct because they weren't being pollinated. Sometimes insects such as bees can take over a bird's pollinating job if the bird disappears. But certain birds are better pollinators than bees are for some plants and are hard to replace if they disappear from the ecosystem.

Scientists estimate that birds pollinate as many as 75 agricultural or medicinal plant species. That scarlet bee balm the ruby-throated hummingbird pollinated is a

Like all sunbirds, the brown-throated sunbird in southeast Asia has a curved bill that helps it sip nectar from flowers. It's a good pollinator of wild bananas.
MOMNOI/GETTY IMAGES

The long bills of hummingbirds are particularly well designed for reaching inside scarlet bee-balm flowers for nectar.
CHRIS ALCOCK/SHUTTERSTOCK.COM

popular garden plant. Bee-balm teas and medicines have been used for a long time by some Indigenous Peoples. Your parents might be interested to know that the mouthwash they use could contain an ingredient from a bee-balm plant that was pollinated by a hummingbird.

STINKY GOLD

Would you be surprised if I told you that bird poop is worth money? Guano is the name for large accumulations of bird poop. It's one of nature's best fertilizers. Those swallow droppings on my deck are high in nitrogen, phosphorus and other nutrients good for the plants in my garden. In areas where thousands of seabirds gather in what's called a colony, their poop builds up over time into giant guano piles. Imagine the stink! But in the mid-1800s, before the invention of synthetic (human-made) fertilizers, guano piles were mined like gold and were worth almost as much. Even today some natural fertilizers available in garden stores include guano. When I clean up the swallow poop on my deck, I happily mix it into my compost bin for the garden.

But guano is worth much more than money. The effect of guano on islands in the Gulf of Mexico is a good example of how in nature everything is connected to everything else. The birds that nest on the islands eat fish in the surrounding ocean and then fly into the trees to roost or nest. There they drop guano on the ground. The guano provides nutrients to the plants under the tree. The plants grow taller and lusher. But because the ocean has become polluted with human garbage, there are fewer fish for the birds to eat. The birds have fewer chicks. Fewer birds means less guano for the plants, so there are fewer plants. In this way, the health of the ocean affects the health of the *food web* on land.

Pelicans, penguins and other birds nesting on the Ballestas Islands reserve off the south coast of Peru produce a lot of white, nutrient-rich guano. SVILUPPO/SHUTTERSTOCK.COM

BUGS ON THE MENU

In 1958 the Chinese government declared an all-out war on sparrows because they were eating grain from the fields. During the Great Sparrow Campaign, people from all over China banged pots to keep the sparrows from landing. The exhausted birds eventually fell dead to the ground. Other people destroyed nests, broke eggs, killed chicks and shot sparrows from the sky. So many birds died that locusts, one of the insects sparrows had been eating, increased in large numbers. With no sparrows to eat them, the locusts destroyed the rice and grain crops that people relied on for food. The Great Sparrow Campaign was one of the causes of the Great Chinese Famine (1958–1961), which killed millions of people.

Birds that eat insects are called insectivores. They help keep insect populations in check in forests, grasslands and other ecosystems, so the insects don't eat everything in sight or spread disease. Insect-eating birds also help control agricultural pests and reduce the number of problem insects like mosquitos and wasps in your backyard and garden.

Some types of birds, including swallows, flycatchers, warblers and woodpeckers, munch on insects for most of their diet. In fact, over half of all bird species eat insects and other invertebrates. They snatch them out of the air while flying, pick them off leaves and out of the soil, drill them from tree bark and scoop them up while swimming.

Farmers around the world have learned that providing food and habitat for the birds that eat the insects that harm their crops benefits both the farmer and the birds.

CLEANUP CREW

On my husband's birthday a few years ago, we discovered six turkey vultures sitting in our yard. We joked that they'd heard Gary was getting old. Turkey vultures are scavengers of carrion (dead animals). Sounds gruesome. But Gary is a good sport and loved the black humor. He also appreciates the role vultures play in nature. Like the people who collect the garbage your family produces, scavenger birds such as vultures and condors act as natural cleanup crews. By eating rotting carrion, they perform an

Turkey vultures can find their carrion dinners by smell alone.
TONY CAMPBELL/SHUTTERSTOCK.COM

Vultures eat carrion at a Jatayu restaurant (feeding station) run by a local community in Nepal. TULSI R SUBEDI

important health service, preventing the spread of disease to humans and animals. Juices in the stomach of vultures are so acidic they destroy disease-causing bacteria and viruses. In cultures such as India's, where the dead are not buried but laid out on the ground or in trees, scavengers are revered for their spiritual role in helping the souls of the dead fly to heaven.

Vulture populations have been declining fast in Africa, Asia and Europe. The birds are poisoned by drugs used to treat sick livestock and die from lack of food and collisions with wind turbines and power lines. As vultures disappear from the landscape, carrion builds up. Stray dogs have taken over the scavenging job and are growing in number. They spread the dangerous rabies virus to humans.

The role of vultures as ecosystem cleanup crews is so important in many places that there is now an International Vulture Awareness Day. Held on the first Saturday in September, this event helps educate people about the importance of vultures and how to protect them.

FEATHERED LANDLORDS

Large, exotic-looking pileated woodpeckers with their bright-red crests live in the forest behind my home. I hear them rat-a-tat-tatting on tree trunks (or sometimes my house!). It's hard to believe how fast they peck—up to 20 times per second.

Why do woodpeckers peck (drum)? They do it to communicate with other woodpeckers, to say "This is my territory" or to attract a mate. Woodpeckers and sapsuckers (a species of woodpecker) peck in order to feed on insects or sap, create a nest cavity or store food like acorns and seeds. There are about 214 known

TWEETS FROM THE FLYWAY

The pattern of holes can tell you what kind of woodpecker made them. Pileated woodpeckers make large deep rectangular holes and leave piles of wood chips on the ground. Sapsuckers drill sap wells—horizontal rows of tiny holes that fill with sap. Hairy, downy and red-bellied woodpeckers tear off bark and make a wavy pattern of small holes in the trunk as they search for insects.

A yellow-bellied sapsucker.
JAMES PINTAR/DREAMSTIME.COM

species of woodpeckers in the world, and they all make holes. The holes benefit other species. Fungi and insects move in and speed up the decomposition of the wood. Hummingbirds feed on the sap that drips from the holes made by sapsuckers.

Woodpeckers make a new nest every year. Once they're done with the old ones, other birds and animals use them. Like a food web, a nest web, where many different species are connected by the nests they make and leave behind for others, often starts with a woodpecker making a hole. Ten percent of all birds and vertebrates use cavities for nesting or feeding. When a forest has lots of woodpeckers, you know the habitat is good for lots of other species. High-quality woodpecker habitat indicates high ecological value.

It's fun to watch woodpeckers going about their business. That's why they are good for the local economy too, attracting bird-watchers from near and far.

A POEM AS LOVELY AS A BIRD

A long time ago in Australia—some think as far back as 40,000 years ago—someone used red ochre, a pigment made from iron oxide, to paint a 20-foot (6-meter)-tall picture of a bird on a rock wall. That's the height of three or four people standing on one another's shoulders! The bird, *Genyornis newtoni*, is extinct now, but the painting still exists: it was discovered in 2008. It tells us that humans have valued birds for a long time.

Appreciating birds for their artistic value is an example of a cultural ecosystem service. Culture is the language, religion, foods, social habits, music and arts that make one group of people in a society distinct from others.

Genyornis, an extinct "thunder bird" of Australia, was important enough as a cultural icon that the government put it on a stamp.
NEFTALI/SHUTTERSTOCK.COM

Do you think the Beijing National Stadium looks like an upside-down bird's nest? ALEX CIMBAL/SHUTTERSTOCK.COM

Birds contribute to the cultures of societies around the world. They have inspired the creation of art, music and literature. Bird-related recreation and tourism benefit us by improving our physical and mental health, making us feel happy. Birds have even inspired science and technology. For example, zippers mimic the ability of bird feathers to hook together. The aerodynamic high-speed bullet train in Japan was inspired by the sight of a kingfisher diving into a pond without a splash. Beijing National Stadium, built for the Olympics in 2008, was designed to mimic the shape of an upside-down bird's nest. Creations that imitate or are inspired by nature are examples of biomimicry.

Cultural services give us a sense of belonging to a group. In Canada, where I live, thousands of people voted to name the Canada jay as the country's national bird, as a symbol of what it means to be Canadian. Guatemala's national bird, the resplendent quetzal, is such an important cultural symbol that the country's money is called the quetzal. Does your country, state or province have an official symbolic bird?

The long-tailed resplendent quetzal is not only Guatemala's national bird but also the name of that country's money. FJZEA/SHUTTERSTOCK.COM

CANARY IN THE COAL MINE

You may have heard the phrase "canary in the coal mine." This refers to a time when canaries were kept in cages deep down in coal mines. If the canary died, the miners knew oxygen was getting low and they needed to return to the surface for fresh air.

This practice wasn't good for the canary, but the story illustrates how birds can be excellent *bioindicators* (gauges of ecosystem health). They live in almost every type of environment, they are easy to see and observe, and we know quite a lot about them. Many eat at the top of the food chain, so their health can tell us something about the health of their prey (what they eat) or the ecosystem they live in.

For example, if the population of shearwaters (a species of fish-eating seabird) is healthy, we know there are lots of sand lance, their main fish prey, in the ocean. Some bird species are very sensitive to certain chemicals. Bird death, illness or the thinning of their eggshells can alert us to the presence of invisible environmental pollutants in their food or in the air, soil or water. Mapping changes in where birds live and in their populations can tell scientists about changes in climate.

In these ways, birds can act as early warning systems for environmental problems that may soon affect other species, including us.

Coal miners relied on canaries to indicate the presence of lethal gases deep down in the mines.
PUBLIC DOMAIN

YOUNG BIRDERS

Mliss Turgeon started birding at a young age on her family acreage in northern Ontario. Mliss loves identifying birds and is great at recognizing birdcalls. She's especially talented at capturing the beauty of birds in her drawings, paintings and photographs. Mliss enjoys learning about bird behavior and how birds can be encouraged to thrive in their natural habitats. Some of her favorite birds are hummingbirds, warblers, kinglets and loons.

JP

The eastern meadowlark, a common songbird whose range extends from eastern North America to South America, is disappearing fast because its grassland and prairie habitat is disappearing too.
STEVE BYLAND/DREAMSTIME.COM

5

BEATING THE BIG BAD THREE

WHERE HAS ALL THE BIRD LIFE GONE?

There's no doubt about it: birds are beautiful, intelligent animals, valuable to both nature and humans. But many birds worldwide are in trouble. The International Union for the Conservation of Nature (IUCN), an organization that keeps track of how the world's plants and animals are doing, has listed about 13 percent of all bird species (almost 1,400 species) on its Red List. A bird species is placed on that list because it's threatened with extinction. That's 1 in 8 bird species that will disappear from the planet unless something is done very soon to save them. Almost 200 bird species are listed as critically endangered, and they don't have much time left.

Even many common birds have declined in population in recent decades. The number of barn swallows like the ones that nest on my deck decreased by 95 percent in North America in the last 40 years.

TWEETS FROM THE FLYWAY

The populations of many common birds are declining quickly. A team of scientists from the North American Bird Conservation Initiative studied the issue and made a list of 33 common bird species in the United States whose numbers are rapidly decreasing. The world population of many of these species has dropped by half in 40 years. Some species of gulls, owls, swallows, sparrows, warblers and ducks are on this list.

The population of endangered forest owlets has declined to about 250 birds because of loss and degradation of their forest habitat in India.
AUGGIEFERNS/SHUTTERSTOCK.COM

And the total number of hummingbirds, the ones that sip from my feeders and migrate to Mexico every summer, decreased by 62 percent in the past 50 years. Just imagine for a moment what your neighborhood would be like if the wild birds disappeared. My deck might be cleaner, but I know my neighborhood would be a lot quieter, with less movement and color. And, as you learned in chapter 3, without birds the earth would be a much poorer, less healthy place for all of us.

To change things for the better, we must first understand the causes of the problem. Have you heard the term *ecological footprint*? It's a measure of the effect each of us has on nature, such as how much water we use or how much pollution we produce. It applies to our effect on birds too. Everything we do has consequences, and many have proven to be harmful to birds, even if unintended.

Scientists have made a long list of problems that threaten birds. The top three are habitat loss, *invasive species* and *climate change*. Read on to find out how the big bad three affect birds and learn what you can do, no matter where you live and no matter how old you are, to reduce your ecological footprint as it relates to birds. And remember, what's good for birds is good for people too—clean air, water and food, and safe, healthy homes.

PAVING PARADISE AND PUTTING UP A PARKING LOT

The forest owlet is an oddball. Unlike most owls, which hunt at night, the forest owlet likes to sunbathe, especially when the weather is cool. It lives in dry forests in central India. But illegal tree cutting and clearing for agriculture have reduced the habitat the owls need. They are now critically endangered. Only 50 to 250 forest owlets are left in the wild.

When we clear land for buildings, farms, roads, parking lots, mines, factories or other human uses—which is called *ecosystem conversion*—natural habitat for wildlife is gone forever. We'll never get it back. Where I live, in an area called the Coastal Douglas-Fir Zone of British Columbia, more than half of the natural habitat has been permanently converted for human use. Much of the rest continues to be damaged and divided, or fragmented, into smaller and smaller areas by logging, mining and other development. There's not much left for the birds and other native animals and plants.

According to one estimate, only 15 percent of habitat around the world is still in a natural, pristine condition, unaffected by human activity. When the forests, grasslands

Birds lose out when forest habitat is replaced by monoculture, such as palm oil plantations. Palm oil is in baked goods, candy, shampoo, cosmetics, cleaning agents, washing detergents, toothpaste and more. TAMI616/GETTY IMAGES

and wetlands that provide food and shelter are gone, wildlife must move somewhere else to find them. Around the world, bird species like the forest owlet are being squeezed into smaller and smaller places as their habitat is lost and fragmented. For many birds, there is nowhere else to go.

Some birds live well in habitats that have been converted for human use. There were no house sparrows in North America before 1852, when 16 birds were introduced to Brooklyn, New York, from England. Now there are millions of the city-loving sparrows. But even the adaptable house sparrow is feeling the crush of the human footprint. In recent years house sparrow populations have plummeted in North America, as well as in Australia, India and especially in Europe. Why? No one knows.

Imagine walking by a farmer's field. You see lots of birds flying around or feeding on the ground. It's natural to think the habitat looks healthy and has always been that way. You find out later that the field was once a forest that provided a home for a larger number of birds and a greater variety of bird species than it does today. How do you see that farmer's field now? Judging an ecosystem's health on the basis of what we see now instead of what it used to be is called shifting baseline syndrome. When we don't recognize what has been lost, we may falsely believe that all is well. As a result, we might carry on with activities that are harmful to birds and other wildlife.

THINK LIKE A BIRD

Even a home garden represents a loss of natural habitat. There are lots of things your family can do to make your yard (if you have one) more bird-friendly. Schoolyards too. Start by thinking like a bird! What do birds need to

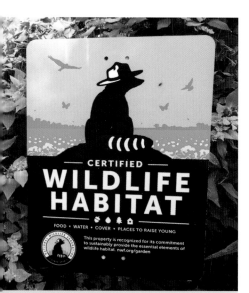

In the United States, if your garden provides food, water, cover and places for birds and other wildlife to raise their young, and is managed using sustainable practices, you can apply to have it designated a Certified Wildlife Habitat by the National Wildlife Federation under its Gardens for Wildlife program. Check out the NWF's Native Plant Finder to learn which native plants are best for supporting birds in your area.
NATIONAL WILDLIFE FEDERATION

survive and thrive? Food, water, shelter and a place to nest. Planting native plants is a simple way to provide habitat for resident and migratory birds. Check out the Audubon Society's Plants for Birds program to find lists of native plants suitable for your area. Join the society's campaign to plant one million bird-friendly plants across North America. Hummingbirds, for example, don't need artificial nectar feeders if they have a continuous supply of native flowers to feed on. Grow plants organically, without pesticides that might be toxic to birds.

Gardens often don't contain trees old enough to have natural nesting cavities, so putting up nest boxes, roosting towers and nesting platforms will provide homes for birds. Maintain natural wetlands and sources of water like ponds or streams. If there aren't any, provide water in a birdbath or other container so birds can bathe or drink on hot summer days. Just as with feeders, keep the water

TWEETS FROM THE FLYWAY

Guerrilla gardeners secretly plant gardens on vacant public or private land without permission. They do it to make a statement about the way the land is being used, and to grow food for humans or provide habitat for wildlife, including birds and butterflies. A simple "seed bomb" of native plant seeds, thrown from a bike or car into bare soil, is a popular way to start one. Guerrilla gardens are popping up in North America, Europe, the United Kingdom, Australia and New Zealand. In some places, guerrilla gardening has led to changes in policies and laws to allow the legal gardening of boulevards and vacant lots for the benefit of birds and other wildlife (including us!).

fresh and clean, providing new water and cleaning out containers every day if needed.

One piece of advice about bird-friendly gardening that I particularly like is to be messy. When my neighbors complain about my gardening habits, I can educate them by telling them, "It's for the birds." Bird-friendly gardening means leaving dead flower heads so the seeds can be eaten by finches and sparrows. It means keeping a brush pile in your yard so that birds have a place in which to hide, play or nest, and it means shrinking that lawn or getting rid of it completely. Birds prefer forest and meadows. The more your family garden or schoolyard looks like natural habitat, the more feeding, perching, nesting and hiding places birds will find.

Creating bird-friendly gardens connects people with nature and can inspire us to do more. Don't forget about the birds that don't come to feeders or your yard. Some of these are the species most in trouble, like seabirds, shorebirds and tropical forest birds. Many bird lovers are inspired to make changes in their lives that benefit birds, and work with others to take conservation action to improve and save habitat for birds and other wildlife.

BUYING FOR THE BIRDS

Do you like chocolate as much as I do? You might be surprised to know that buying the right kind of chocolate can help birds. Cocoa, the main ingredient for making chocolate, comes from cocoa beans. Cocoa beans grow on cacao, a tropical plant grown mostly in Africa and South America. Other crops cultivated in these regions often require forest to be cut down so the plants have enough sun. There goes the bird habitat. But cacao grows best in the shade, under the forest canopy. Cacao is a good crop for farmers to grow and sell because it doesn't require the forest to be cut down. Both the farmer and the birds benefit—the farmers can make a living, and the rainforest is preserved for birds and other wildlife. Studies have shown that shade-grown cacao plantations have as much biodiversity as natural, untouched forests.

Buying chocolate made from "rustic" cacao planted in the shade of tropical forests can help provide habitat for endangered birds like the ochraceous attila, a flycatcher that lives in Colombia, Ecuador and Peru. NICK ATHANAS

Another benefit is that shade-grown plants require no chemical pesticides or fertilizers. Next time you want a chocolate bar, make sure it's from a company that uses only shade-grown organic cacao. Even better, buy *fair trade* products to ensure that the people who grow the cacao are paid fairly for their work. Some chocolate companies donate some of their profits to species and habitat conservation.

Coffee is another tropical plant that can be grown in the sun or the shade. Vast areas of tropical forest that provide wildlife habitat are cut down to plant sun-grown coffee. The plantations require lots of fertilizers and pesticides. You may not drink coffee, but if the adults in your life do,

TWEETS FROM THE FLYWAY

Some organizations certify chocolate and coffee products so that consumers know the ingredients in their purchases are grown or made in a way that doesn't harm the environment or people. Certification means that cacao and coffee plants are grown using organic methods and without pesticides or chemical fertilizers. They are grown under the shade of a variety of native trees, so that there's lots of different habitat for birds and other wildlife. Look for certification labels such as Rainforest Alliance, Bird Friendly Smithsonian, Organic or Fair Trade on chocolate and coffee packaging.

THE SMITHSONIAN INSTITUTION
RAINFOREST ALLIANCE
FAIRTRADE
US DEPARTMENT OF AGRICULTURE

suggest they help birds out by drinking only shade-grown, organic coffee.

With seven billion people living on the planet, other consumer choices can have a huge impact on the environment, including on birds. Using sustainable lumber and paper products made from trees harvested selectively or from recycled materials will help prevent forest loss. Avoiding beef grown on tropical rainforest land cleared for pasture is another simple action you can take to prevent the loss of bird habitat. Look for supermarkets and fast-food restaurants that sell beef from cattle grown on native grasslands, where grazing sustains vital habitat for the most endangered grassland birds.

Millions more acres of tropical forest have been cleared in Malaysia and Indonesia to plant oil palms. Palm oil is commonly used for cooking in many Asian countries, but it's also an ingredient in up to 50 percent of commercial food and household items sold around the world, including potato chips, chocolate, cookies, margarine, dishwashing liquid, shampoo and lipstick. Smartphone apps like PalmSmart in Canada and the United States and Palm Oil Investigations (POI) in Australia and New Zealand make it easier for you to know whether a product contains palm oil. Look for products labeled *Palm Oil Free*.

STRANGER DANGER

The forests of Guam, an island off the coast of the Philippines, are eerily devoid of bird sounds. Shortly after World War II, brown tree snakes were accidentally introduced to the island—they'd hitched rides from the South Pacific in the cargo of American military planes, unknown to the human crew. With no natural predators around, the snakes multiplied and ate almost every egg, nestling and adult bird in sight. Within a few decades they had wiped out all but three of the 14 native bird species on the island. Gone from the island are the Micronesian kingfisher, the Mariana fruit dove and the rufous fantail. The endemic Guam rail was saved from extinction only

Thousands of invasive brown tree snakes in Guam have eaten almost all the native birds. GORDON H. RODDA/ US FISH AND WILDLIFE SERVICE

TWEETS FROM THE FLYWAY

Sometimes birds are invasive species too. For example, barred owls that are native to eastern Canada have moved west, where they have become a threat to some species. Near my forest home, I enjoy observing the newly arrived barred owls and hearing their *who-cooks-for-youuu* calls, but, sadly, they have driven out the smaller western screech owls native to this area. My friend Tania Tripp, a wildlife biologist and owl whisperer, works with other biologists and community groups (including mine) to install nest boxes with entrance holes too small for the barred owls. The program is encouraging the screech owls to safely nest again in the forests they used to live in before the barred owls arrived. The boxes also provide a nesting place for the screech owls in forests where logging has cut down the old trees, which have the best natural nesting cavities.

Wildlife biologist Tania Tripp invented this handy-dandy camera on a pole to check on the use of nest boxes by western screech owls. ANN ERIKSSON

The invasive barred owl is beautiful but has displaced the native western screech owls from the forests near my home. TONY CAMPBELL/SHUTTERSTOCK.COM

due to human efforts to breed it in captivity and release the young on a neighboring island, but the endemic Guam flycatcher is now extinct—gone forever. Even dropping thousands of poison-filled mice from planes hasn't gotten rid of the snakes.

Without birds around to eat insects, spider populations have exploded. And because seed-eating birds are gone, few new trees are growing in the forest. So far, no one has been able to think of a solution to this problem. If you become an ornithologist, maybe you will!

The human species, *Homo sapiens*, first appeared on earth about 300,000 years ago—the blink of an eye in comparison to the 150 million years birds have been here. In that short time, we've spread out around the planet. When we move, we often take our favorite plants or animals with us, for food or pleasure. And sometimes we don't know we have hitchhikers moving along with us in the form of seeds stuck to our clothes or to the tires of our vehicles—or, as with the brown tree snakes, in shipments of goods traveling around the world. A plant or animal that ends up in a habitat in which it doesn't normally live is called an exotic or introduced species. When introduced species cause problems in their new habitat, they are considered invasive. Habitat loss and fragmentation and changes in climate have also created opportunities for invasive species to move in to new areas. Invasive animals compete for food and shelter with wild birds or eat them. Introduced plants can displace the native food plants that birds rely on.

FATAL FELINES

You might be surprised to hear that your pet is an invasive species. Cats, introduced into natural habitats by humans, prey on birds and bird eggs. Cats are considered one of the 100 worst invasive species in the world. In fact, in the United States and Canada, they are the number one directly human-caused threat to birds. In the United States alone, free-roaming domestic cats and feral cats with no owners kill about 2.4 billon birds—ground-nesting, foraging and songbirds—every year! Many of these birds are already endangered because of other factors.

Cats are natural predators. You've probably played with a cat using a piece of string or yarn. Stalking and pouncing during play are examples of predatory behavior. Even well-fed cats will hurt and kill birds. During one study, one-third of cats fitted with a video camera were shown to kill one animal, including birds, for every 17 hours they were outside. Some cat owners hang bells around the necks of their cats, thinking the bell will warn birds away. But studies have shown that cats wearing bells kill as many (or more!) birds than cats without bells. Researchers think

Mute swans were initially brought to North America from Europe, starting in the mid-1800s, to decorate ponds and lakes in towns and cities. They've now spread into the wild, where they disturb ecosystems, displace native species and are sometimes aggressive to humans. JANET GRIFFIN-SCOTT/SHUTTERSTOCK.COM

it's because birds are warned by the sight of a cat, not the sound. Cats might also learn to walk more stealthily so the bell doesn't ring.

Cats are responsible for killing many endangered and migratory birds that are protected by law under the international Migratory Bird Treaty Act and the Endangered Species Act in the United States. Technically, cat owners are breaking the law by allowing their pets to roam free and harm birds. Cats also carry diseases such as the parasite *Toxoplasma gondii*, which can spread to birds and other wildlife—and people. Feral cats have caused the extinction of 33 bird species worldwide.

CAT CONTROL

People love their cats. Perhaps you have one yourself. Cats can be wonderful companions. Studies show that having a pet is good for our mental health. But if free-roaming cats are not good for birds, what's the solution?

The American Bird Conservancy (ABC) says we should keep cats indoors. But aren't cats meant to roam outside? Isn't it unhealthy for them to be indoors all the time? In fact, indoor cats are happier and healthier than cats allowed outside. Indoor cats don't get injured by cars or dogs or fights with other cats. They have fewer parasites and diseases than outdoor cats. Join other bird lovers to help protect birds and the health of your pet by taking ABC's online pledge to keep cats safely contained. Then follow these simple recommendations from ABC to make sure your indoor cat is happy.

- Provide places such as windowsills or shelves where cats can sit and see outside.
- Play with your cat every day and provide toys such as paper bags and cardboard boxes so they can entertain themselves while you are away.

When your cat is kept indoors, both the cat and the bird are safe. Outdoor cats live an average of 2 to 3 years, while indoor cats can live for 15 to 20.
ANDRZEJ PUCHTA/SHUTTERSTOCK.COM

- Plant kitty grass in indoor planters for your cat to munch on.
- If your family is able to, provide your cat with a safe outdoor enclosure such as a screened porch.
- Keep the litter box clean.
- Take your cat to the vet regularly.
- If you find a feral cat, take it to a local animal shelter for adoption to a good home where people understand that a healthy cat is an indoor cat.

WINDS OF CHANGE

In the summer of 2017, the island community in which I live was invaded by dozens of Steller's jays, a species rarely seen here. About six of the large, crested blue-black birds hung out in my yard until winter. They acted like a noisy, boisterous pack of teenagers goofing around. They chased other birds from the feeders. I wondered why the jays suddenly appeared. It turned out they'd been displaced by wildfires hundreds of miles away, as one of the worst wildfire seasons in my part of the world was in 2017. The fires are suspected to be the result of changes in the climate.

Steller's jays are not endangered, but they are still affected by the changing climate.
TIM ZUROWSKI/SHUTTERSTOCK.COM

You've likely heard the terms *climate change* and *global warming*. Burning fossil fuels such as oil, gasoline, coal and natural gas to drive our cars, heat and cool our homes, and produce and transport all the stuff we use produces carbon dioxide and other gases like methane. The gases are released into the troposphere, the narrow blanket of gases in the earth's atmosphere that makes life possible. The clearing of land for agriculture and the raising of cattle and other animals for meat also contribute huge amounts of carbon dioxide and methane. These *greenhouse gases* trap heat in the atmosphere. As more and more greenhouse gases are released, the planet warms. So far the planet has warmed about 1.8 degrees Fahrenheit (1 degree Celsius), and it is expected to get warmer as more greenhouse gases are released. This global warming is causing the earth's long-term climate to change. The local weather is becoming more unpredictable. There are more frequent and bigger storms, heavier rains, longer droughts and greater extremes of cold and heat. Global warming is also causing the ocean to warm and sea levels to rise. The changing climate is already affecting many wild birds, such as the Steller's jays who fled the drought-fueled fires and ended up in my yard. Nearly one-quarter of 570 bird species that have been studied are having problems related to climate change.

Too Hot for Comfort

Two researchers from Cornell University have discovered that 87 bird species in New Guinea are moving higher up the mountain to find their preferred habitat as temperatures increase from global warming. Four species are already at the top of the mountain and have nowhere to go if temperatures keep rising as expected.

This upward movement of birds is one of the results of climate change that scientists and birders are noticing. Bird species are also moving north because temperatures in the south are becoming too warm for them and the habitat they need. If you've been bird-watching for a few years, you might notice birds appearing where they aren't expected to be.

Climate change is causing other problems for birds too. More frequent and bigger storms, heat waves or cold snaps

The Audubon Society's climate model predicts that the brown pelican will lose over half of its current winter range along the coast of North America by the year 2080. No one knows what climate change will do to the fish the pelicans eat.
JIM CUMMING/SHUTTERSTOCK.COM

can kill birds not used to the severe conditions or displace them from their usual homes. After a huge storm in 2013, bird-watchers in the United Kingdom were amazed to see birds such as Cape May warblers and ruby-crowned kinglets from North America and White's thrush from Siberia. The tiny birds had been blown thousands of miles from their home.

Sea-level rise might flood habitat important to birds. People in Costa Rica are worried that mangrove forests, critical habitat for mangrove hummingbirds, might disappear as sea level rises. The world's landscape might change in other ways over time as the climate changes. For example, forests might become grasslands, meaning birds living there would no longer find the food plants or insects they need.

Birds already under threat and declining from habitat loss or invasive species are expected to face new or bigger stresses from climate change. While climate change may not be the most immediate threat to most birds right now, scientists expect it to affect many species in the future.

TWEETS FROM THE FLYWAY

Climate change is affecting birds even in the most remote regions of earth. The number of penguins in Baily Head in the northern part of Antarctica dropped from 85,000 breeding pairs to 52,000 in just 7 years. In the last 75 years, the average temperature in the Antarctic Peninsula has increased by almost three times the average elsewhere on the planet. This rapid warming causes the air to carry more moisture and is bringing more rain to the nesting sites of penguins that need cold, dry weather for their eggs to hatch. To make matters worse, the penguin's main food source, *zooplankton* called krill, is disappearing along with the melting sea ice. Scientists worry that the warming waters will move south and cause the same problems in other penguin colonies.

Chinstrap penguins at Baily Head, Antarctica. PASCALINE DANIEL/SHUTTERSTOCK.COM

The mature hardwood forests in the eastern United States that cerulean warblers depend on in the summer are expected to shift northward from their current location because of climate change. But will the warbler's forest habitat be able to adapt and move as fast as the changing conditions or will it decline?
RAY HENNESSY/SHUTTERSTOCK.COM

TWEETS FROM THE FLYWAY

Some flocks of migrating birds are so enormous that they show up on radar. So many birds migrate along flyways in spring and fall that their migration has been described like an hourglass—the northern hemisphere empties of birds in the autumn and fills up again in the spring.

Mismatch

Every year in August my family and I love to pick blackberries to munch on, bake or freeze for later. When we arrived at our favorite picking spot in the summer of 2017, we discovered that the berries had shriveled up in the unusually hot and dry weather. We went home hungry and empty-handed. Some birds are starting to have the same problem, returning from winter migration too late to take advantage of their preferred food because it has dried up, bloomed, hatched or left earlier than usual because of the changing climate. Scientists describe this problem in timing as *mismatch*.

Mismatch is the reason Cassin's auklets, seabirds that breed on Triangle Island, not far from where I live, are having fewer chicks. Why? They eat tiny animals in the ocean called zooplankton, which aren't around in big enough numbers anymore at the time the auklets need them. Seabirds might be most at risk of mismatch because their prey relies on certain ocean temperatures and currents, both of which have been changing rapidly because of global warming.

It's not all bad news though. Climate change might be good for some birds, giving them a longer warm season in which to breed and raise their chicks. Great tits in the United Kingdom are laying their eggs about two weeks earlier than before to match the earlier hatching of moth caterpillars, their favorite food.

Some birds might help reduce or mitigate (make less severe) the effects of climate change on humans. For example, insect-eating birds might eat problem insects such as disease-carrying mosquitoes that move into areas as temperatures rise.

TWEETS FROM THE FLYWAY

Canadian Katya Kondratyuk's enthusiasm for birding is contagious! She started birding at age 11. Right away other birders noticed how sharp she was at spotting birds. Katya sends her photos and sightings to eBird, the Birding in BC forum (Birding.bc.ca) and her Flickr page. She's also a citizen scientist, participating every year in the Christmas Bird Count for Kids. The Christmas Bird Count (CBC) is a North American program of the Audubon Society and Bird Studies Canada. CBC records going back more than 100 years help scientists learn about the health of bird populations over time and decide what conservation actions might be needed. Bird counts help scientists track changes in the timing of migrations, how and where diseases are affecting birds, and how the species and number of birds in different habitats might be changing. In 2014 the Audubon Society used the CBC data to publish its first *Birds and Climate Change* report. It concluded that over half of the 588 North American birds scientists studied may soon be in trouble due to climate change.

MELISSA HAFTING

WALK TO SCHOOL, SAVE A BIRD

It might be hard to believe, but walking or riding your bike to school instead of riding in a car can benefit wild birds. Any action that reduces the amount of greenhouse gases going into the atmosphere will help slow down climate change and its harmful impacts on birds. Put on a sweater instead of turning up the heat, or sit in the shade instead of running the air conditioner. Turn off lights when you don't need them. Write that school assignment with a paper and pen instead of using the computer. Plant a carbon-absorbing tree (or many).

This gull is encouraging the car's owner to do the environment a favor by walking instead of driving.
KARKHUT/SHUTTERSTOCK.COM

The shade-grown chocolate and coffee you learned about in chapter 3 do more than save habitat. They also help prevent the cutting down of millions of carbon-absorbing trees. In the same way, choosing not to eat beef saves trees that would otherwise be cut down to create pastures for cattle grazing. It also helps reduce the release of the greenhouse gas methane from more than a billion farting, belching animals. Shipping food and other goods long distances by freighter, airplane, train and truck spews a lot of greenhouse gases into the atmosphere. Choose foods that travel few *food miles*, such as items grown or produced locally (maybe in your backyard).

Being energy efficient is another solution for tackling the climate-change problem. The watt is the basic unit of energy consumption. The lamp above my desk uses a 40-watt bulb, which means it consumes 40 watts of energy an hour. I love the concept of the negawatt: the amount of energy you *don't* use. If I turn off that lamp for an hour I'll earn 40 megawatts. If I replace it with a 9-watt LED bulb, I'll save 31 watts every hour it's on. Using appliances, electronics, cars and other consumer goods that do more

with less energy may not be as effective as using no energy at all, but these items offer another way to reduce your energy consumption. Look for products labeled Energy Efficient or EnergyStar. If your family can't get by without a car, encourage them to get one that uses less fuel or operates on electricity. An electric car emits no greenhouse gases at all. Electric vehicles are especially helpful at cutting greenhouse gases if the electricity they run on is produced from renewable energy sources like solar, wind, tidal or geothermal.

A word of caution though. We don't yet know how these new forms of energy production will affect birds. So far we haven't invented a way of producing renewable energy that's completely safe for birds. Birds crash into wind turbines. Hydroelectric dams flood habitats and pollute water sources. Tidal power can affect wading birds

One way to prevent birds from being injured and killed by wind turbines is to locate the turbines away from migration paths. BILDAGENTUR ZOONAR GMBH/SHUTTERSTOCK.COM

and waterfowl and interrupt migration patterns along flyways. Bioenergy crops like corn and sugarcane for making liquid fuels can be sources of pesticides and need large amounts of land to produce. The production of all forms of renewable energy results in habitat loss and fragmentation. Of all the current technologies, rooftop solar energy may have the least impact on birds, but the issue hasn't been well studied. Birds have collided with large solar structures, and they have been burned in solar arrays (groups of solar panels), which act like mirrors. The mining of materials for solar panels and batteries also removes habitat, causes pollution and produces greenhouse gases. Maybe you can think of a way to produce energy that won't harm birds. And don't forget those negawatts, the most bird-friendly option of all.

By 2070 European bee-eaters might have to fly an extra 4.5 days and 1,600 miles (1,000 kilometers) to travel between their breeding and nonbreeding habitats because of climate change. JAKLZDENEK/SHUTTERSTOCK.COM

EC SIA

Search the web to plant trees...

TWEETS FROM THE FLYWAY

Surf the Web to combat climate change and create bird habitat. What? Doesn't online browsing use energy and create more greenhouse gases? It usually does, but a business in Germany called Ecosia has created a search engine that's helping counteract the impact of internet use. Eighty percent of Ecosia's advertising profits go into planting trees—one tree for every 45 internet searches. By the spring of 2019, Ecosia had planted more than 52 million trees in biodiversity hot spots (regions where biodiversity is significantly threatened) in Burkina Faso, Madagascar, Peru, Indonesia, Morocco, Brazil, Nicaragua, Ethiopia, Tanzania and many other countries. Ecosia's goal is a billion trees by 2020! In 40 years each tree will have stored up to one ton (0.9 metric ton) of carbon dioxide. Planting trees combats climate change and creates habitat for forest birds. It also provides local communities with food, clean air and water, and an income from tree-planting they can use to improve their health care and education. As an added bonus, Ecosia's servers work on 100 percent renewable energy.

ECOSIA.ORG

YOUNG BIRDERS

The Young Birders Club of Uganda educates young people aged 7 to 18 about birds, bird-watching, and protecting and conserving Ugandan birds and their habitats. The club organizes lots of fun field trips around the country. It's nurturing a new generation of enthusiastic and knowledgeable wildlife conservationists. In 2016 club members were able to attend the first-ever African Birding Expo, held in Entebbe. The event brought together people from across Africa and around the world who are interested in everything about birds.

HERBERT BYARUHANGA/UGANDA YOUNG BIRDERS

Katie Warner started birding when she was nine years old and enjoys going on birding trips with the Conejo Valley Audubon Society. She loves birding so much that she wants to be an ornithologist and study birds-of-paradise, colorful rainforest birds that live in Australia, Indonesia and New Guinea. MIHAELA WARNER

6

GIVING WILD BIRDS A BOOST

NO SUCH THING AS "AWAY"

Some wild birds have been able to adapt to the disruption in their lives from habitat loss, invasive species and climate change by moving or finding new food sources. But there's another long list of threats that are impossible to adapt to or escape. Consider the things we throw "away" but that end up in the environment.

Piles of Plastic

Flesh-footed shearwaters are feeding their chicks plastic. Not on purpose. The adults pick up floating pieces of plastic from the Tasman Sea thinking it's food, because it smells like the seaweed they like to eat. The chicks have so much plastic in their stomachs that many are starving. Or they are too weak to fly or swim. One in three flesh-footed shearwaters dies. A team of researchers is trying to help.

Many seabirds, like this pink pelican, mistake plastic trash for food.
MYIMAGES_MICHA/SHUTTERSTOCK.COM

They are catching the chicks and flushing the plastic out of their stomachs to try to give them a chance to survive.

Scientists estimate that 90 percent of seabirds are eating plastic. By 2050 it could be 100 percent. Even in the remote Southern Ocean of Antarctica, seabirds have been found with stomachs full of bags, bottle caps, cigarette lighters, fibers, fishing line and other small bits of plastic. The stomach of one dead bird contained 200 pieces of plastic!

Sharp plastics can puncture the internal organs of birds. Plastic of all kinds can block organs or fill the birds' stomachs so there's no room for the food they need to stay healthy. Seabird populations have dropped by an estimated 67 percent in the last 60 years. Plastic debris is thought to be one of the major causes, killing millions of marine birds every year.

Most plastics are used once and then end up in landfills and the environment. More than 9 billion tons (8.2 billion metric tons) of plastic has been produced in the world since 1950. Only 9 percent has been recycled. Because plastic is not *biodegradable*, every piece produced is still around. Over time it breaks down into smaller and smaller pieces called microplastics, visible only under a microscope.

Items of all sizes end up in the ocean and on land. Plastic debris can entangle birds so they can't eat, swallow, fly or swim. Some plastics are made with toxic chemicals, and water soaks up those toxins, creating another problem for the birds.

Penguins Against Plastic

Kicking our plastic habit is essential if we want to give birds a helping hand. Do a bird a favor and reduce your plastic use by replacing single-use plastic items with reusable alternatives like cloth shopping bags and metal or glass water bottles. Carry reusable or compostable cutlery and bowls with you for takeout food. Ask for a paper straw or no straw at all.

Next time you are out for a walk or a day at the beach, pick up the plastic garbage you see lying around and recycle it or dispose of it responsibly so it won't end up in the environment for birds to eat. If you live near the ocean, watch for organized plastic and trash cleanups, such as the International Coastal Cleanup.

Even recycling is a temporary solution. Some plastic can be recycled only once before it's garbage. Reusing plastic items helps, but those items will still be thrown out one day. Why not stop plastic pollution by refusing to use plastic products at all? I tell my children to think

TWEETS FROM THE FLYWAY

Seabirds are often attracted to fishing boats by the prospect of a free meal of scraps, but this puts them in danger of accidently being caught in fishing gear. Many kinds of birds, fish and other marine species are caught by mistake during fishing seasons, and they often die. The portion of the catch that is unintentional is called bycatch. It's estimated that tens of thousands of seabirds die as bycatch every year. Several organizations, such as the National Seabird Program in the United States, are working on solutions to the problem, such as gear that scares birds away or is weighted to sink deeper in the water. Better management of the waste that attracts birds to fishing boats is helping too.

about what they are going to do with an item they want to purchase when they don't want it anymore. How about a plastic-free family challenge?

Toxic Brew

One day in 1994, three American biologists discovered hundreds of dead Swainson's hawks lying in the road near a field of sunflowers in Argentina. Thousands more of the migratory hawks lay dead between the sunflower rows. The shocked biologists found out that the field had been sprayed with chemicals to kill grasshoppers the farmer believed were harming his crop. Unfortunately, Swainson's hawks love to eat grasshoppers. The hawks literally fell from the sky by the hundreds, poisoned by the highly toxic chemicals coating the insects.

The chemicals used to kill insects or plants that harm food crops and home gardens are called pesticides. They kill not only birds but also the insects many birds rely on for food. A single granule of some pesticides is enough to kill a small bird.

Neonicotinoids, or *neonics*, are pesticides commonly dusted on seeds before planting in order to prevent crop damage by pests. Neonics can stay in soil and water for a long time. You may have heard about the harm neonics are doing to bees. They also harm birds and the insects and worms that birds eat. Neonics make up about one-quarter of the insecticides in use. While it hasn't yet been proven, some scientists believe that neonics have played a big role in the decline of many bird species in recent years. The European Union has temporarily banned the use of neonics, and while bans are being considered in other countries, their use continues.

Swainson's hawks are in danger from pesticides sprayed on crops.
CA2HILL/GETTY IMAGES

Did environmental pollution from crop spraying kill this thrush?
SAULETAS/SHUTTERSTOCK.COM

A farmer sprays insecticide to eradicate crop pests in Boyolali, Central Java, Indonesia. It's not good for the birds, but did you notice that the man is not wearing a mask or gloves to protect himself either? SURYO/DREAMSTIME.COM

Some countries have regulations to control the kinds and amounts of pesticide used, but many countries do not. And regulations are sometimes ignored, or farmers are poorly educated in how to use pesticides and spray too much too often. The crops of greatest risk to birds because of the toxic pesticides used on them are some of the foods we eat a lot of: brussels sprouts, celery, cranberries, cabbage, potatoes, sweet peppers, hot peppers and blueberries. Even in countries with regulations, the massive areas planted with some crops mean that thousands of birds die or are affected by toxic pesticides every year. In the United States, the crops that pose the greatest risk to birds are corn, cotton, alfalfa, wheat and potatoes. Bananas are one of the most highly pesticide-contaminated foods.

Other pollutants silently damage or kill birds. Thousands of birds die every year from small and big oil spills. Birds can't fly, forage, swim or keep warm when they are covered with oil. Even a small amount of oil on a bird's feathers can kill it. Mercury, lead and other toxic pollutants

An oil-covered guillemot in the Netherlands is cleaned at a local bird sanctuary.
COREPICS VOF/SHUTTERSTOCK.COM

pour into the environment every day from industries, farms, gardens, storm drains, vehicles and homes. They don't always kill birds, but they can affect their behavior and disrupt their ability to reproduce and fight off disease. Over time toxins build up in their bodies and cause more serious harm.

SAVE A BIRD—EAT ORGANIC

What's the solution to pesticide damage to birds and bird populations? Save a bird—eat organic is a good motto to live by when it comes to your personal and family food choices. Make your diet more bird-friendly by eating foods grown without the use of chemical pesticides and fertilizers. Choose foods that come from countries and companies that have strong policies to control pesticides and habitat loss. When you go to the store, look at where the foods you wish to purchase are grown, and if they're not labeled, ask the staff.

The production of non-food goods sometimes involves pesticides and other chemicals harmful to birds. The best disposable paper products like toilet paper are the ones

ORGANIC

Smile when you say (and eat!) organic.
The birds you helped will smile too.
RAWPIXEL.COM/SHUTTERSTOCK.COM

This may look like a colorful art piece, but it's really a museum display of 2,100 dead birds killed by tall buildings and recovered by FLAP volunteers in Toronto, ON.
FLAP CANADA/LEIGHTON JONES

made without using chlorine bleach. Biofuels made from corn and other plants are alternatives to fossil fuels. They sound like good choices, but biofuel crops are usually grown with pesticides and fertilizers, and they take up large areas of land too.

Consumer choices that take the health of birds into account may convince producers to create products without using pesticides and other chemicals. Little did the farmer in Argentina know that a healthy population of Swainson's hawks would have helped him by eating millions of grasshoppers in his sunflower fields.

INVISIBLE KILLER

Early in the morning in many cities, people walk around collecting dead and injured birds that have crashed into tall buildings. Seem like a weird thing to do? The people are volunteering for the Fatal Light Awareness Program (FLAP). The nonprofit organization helps raise awareness about the deadly effects of buildings on birds.

In the United States, an estimated 100 million birds a year are killed in collisions with buildings. In Canada, the estimate is 25 million. In the city of Toronto, just 20 tall buildings have killed more than 30,000 birds. In fact, some ornithologists consider collisions with structures a leading cause of bird death in North America. Why? There are two reasons: glass and lights.

Birds can't see glass. When they look at a window they see the reflections of trees, bushes, water or sky— or sometimes the indoor greenery behind the glass. In other words, they see habitat, a safe place to fly to and land. Instead, they hit hard glass, frequently with fatal results. At night the problem is different but no less serious. Migrating birds often travel at night. They may become disoriented by building lights and end up trapped, circling like a moth around a porch light until they drop to the ground, exhausted.

The Audubon Society's Lights Out programs, found in many North American cities, educate people about the dangers to birds that tall buildings, glass and lights pose. The programs encourage building owners to turn out the lights in their buildings during the fall and spring bird migrations. Lights Out saves birds and energy too. FLAP Canada and its many partners have developed BirdSafe, a program dedicated to preventing daytime and nighttime collisions with buildings. The program provides advice and bird-safe standards to homeowners, communities, municipalities and businesses.

Walker Catlett, a member of the Blue Ridge Young Birders Club in Charlottesville, VA, is trying to convince his local YMCA to do something about the problem of birds crashing into their picture windows. His interest in birds is partly why he plans to study environmental conservation and protection. JOANIE EVANS

WINNING OVER WINDOWS

A Cooper's hawk crashed into my bedroom window a few summers ago. Thankfully, the hawk lived, but collisions with windows in my house used to kill more than one bird every year. Maybe your family has the same problem. I decided it was time to bird-proof the windows in our house.

The words on the windows read: "High Impact Visuals", "In Canada, windows kill 25,000,000 birds a year.", "care, reduce the glare! help save lives", "Windows"

Students at the University of Manitoba use art to create awareness about the devastating impact of birds colliding with windows.
ASHA NELSON

The goal is to make all windows visible to birds. Here are some ways to make your windows bird-friendly:

- Place visual markers on the outside of windows. Markers should be at least 1/8 inch (3 millimeters) wide and contrast with the window in all weather conditions. Leave a space between markers that is no more than 2 inches (5 centimeters) wide by 4 inches (10 centimeters) high—ideally 2 inches by 2 inches (5 centimeters by 5 centimeters).

- Cover the windows with stickers that reflect UV light, which birds see but humans don't. Stickers will keep your view unobstructed, but they are expensive and need to be replaced frequently.

- Cover windows with blinds that have slats. An inexpensive alternative to blinds is to hang curtains constructed of thin cord on the outside of windows. I like these because they move in the breeze.

- Keep house plants away from windows so they don't attract birds.

- My all-time favorite bird deterrent, recommended by FLAP Canada's BirdSafe, saves me lots of work. Stop washing the windows and leave them dirty! Even small amounts of dust help reduce reflections.

STOLEN

On the Mediterranean island of Cyprus, hunters illegally trap birds with nets or glue-covered perches called limesticks. In 2016 they killed 2.3 million birds this way in just a few months. Why? The birds are used to make ambelopoulia, a dish made of boiled, grilled, fried or pickled songbirds that is a traditional delicacy in Cyprus. Hunters make millions of dollars every year by selling these birds.

About 120 million birds are hunted and killed every year around the world, sometimes legally, for food, pest control, oil, ingredients for medicines, feathers for decoration, ceremonies and as museum specimens. The illegal catching or killing of animals on someone else's land or in contravention of official protection is called poaching. It's a serious problem that's difficult to control. Poaching can drive a population of birds to extinction. Poachers may not realize (or care) that removing a species of bird from the environment may affect their own families. The birds will no longer be able to pollinate or spread seeds that produce food for the poacher's family.

TWEETS FROM THE FLYWAY

The people in Sivasagar, India, were worried. Protected waterbirds and other threatened species living in the swampy floodplain and open water of the Panidihing Bird Sanctuary were being killed by poachers fishing and hunting illegally. The local people got together and formed a conservation group called Nature's Care and Friend. The group educated residents of villages near the sanctuary about their environment and the importance of protecting the sanctuary and its wild inhabitants. By educating and working with their community, Nature's Care and Friend has successfully reduced the hunting of wading birds and wildfowl such as the greater and lesser adjutant and the swamp francolin.

Lesser adjutant storks are classified as "vulnerable" by the IUCN because of hunting and loss of nesting habitat due to the conversion and degradation of the wetland ecosystems they rely on. JUGAL BHARALI/SHUTTERSTOCK.COM

TWEETS FROM THE FLYWAY

An international treaty called CITES (Convention on International Trade in Endangered Species of Wild Fauna and Flora) has helped slow down the trade of many endangered species. CITES lists plants and animals that can and cannot be traded and under what conditions. But the illegal trafficking of birds and other wildlife still goes on because people still buy them. Grassroots organizations like the Bird Lovers Club, a South Florida nonprofit organization, are working to stop the illegal trade in birds by educating the public. They tell people not to buy baby birds from pet stores unless they know for sure the birds were born and raised in captivity and treated with kindness.

Wild birds such as this Timneh parrot from West Africa may end up in pet stores halfway around the world.
JILL LANG/SHUTTERSTOCK.COM

BIRD IN A SUITCASE

Timneh parrots living in the Bijagós Islands, off the coast of Guinea-Bissua in West Africa, were disappearing. The islands are protected as a biosphere reserve, a special area where researchers study the relationship between people and nature. But the protection wasn't helping the vulnerable parrots, which live only in small areas of West Africa. Poachers were illegally trapping them to be sold as pets in order to make money to support their families. But the World Parrot Trust had a clever idea. They hired people from the local community, including some former parrot trappers, to monitor and protect the Timneh parrot nests. The strategy is paying off. In 2014, with the help of a former poacher turned protector, the first poached chick was returned to its nest and readopted by its parents. This story shows that paying attention to the economic needs of the community, along with education and first-hand engagement with nature, can change people's attitudes and behaviors.

Like poaching, the illegal trafficking of live birds is big business. Slow-breeding birds such as birds of prey (raptors) and parrots are most vulnerable to illegal capture and sale. At least a dozen parrot species are at risk of extinction because of poaching for the illegal pet trade. Most of the 22 species of parrot native to Mexico are affected. Parrots are captured when they are young, and many die or are injured while being smuggled to pet stores or the illegal black market in the United States and other countries.

YOUNG BIRDERS

Six youths under the age of 18 started the not-for-profit society Young Birders New Zealand. They live in different places in the country, but they get together to go birding as often as they can. Every two months they publish an online magazine called *Fledglings NZ*. The magazine is chock-full of fun activities, mind-bending quizzes and fascinating information about New Zealand's amazing birds. Advait Bhave (l) and George Curzon-Hobson (r), members of Young Birders New Zealand, are thankful to see this sign warning them about hunting in the area.

GEORGE CURZON-HOBSON

When many individuals work together, whether they're birds such as these snow geese or people, they can make a big impact. RAY HENNESSY/UNSPLASH.COM

7

KEEPING WILD BIRDS IN FLIGHT

FLOCK TOGETHER FOR CHANGE

Now that you've learned some ways you can help birds on your own or with your family and friends, maybe you feel inspired to do more. People around the world, of all ages, are working together to protect birds and bird habitat. Bird conservation helps entire ecosystems and all the other wildlife that depend on them (including us!).

Have you been fortunate enough to witness a flock of migrating ducks flying in formation, or a cloud of hundreds of starlings whirling around in the sky? They move as if they are one organism, but they are many individual birds working together side by side. In the same way, people working together can achieve great things. Imagine what thousands or millions of people can do for the health of birds by cleaning up harmful plastics or by campaigning together to protect bird habitat. People Power is Bird Power!

When you first start birding, it's helpful to learn from an experienced birder.
KALI9/GETTY IMAGES

CELEBRATE BIRDS

World Migratory Bird Day (WMBD) celebrates birds in the world's three major migratory flyways: the African–Eurasian, East Asian–Australasian and the Americas. In Canada and the United States, WMBD is usually the second Saturday in May. In Mexico, Central and South America, and the Caribbean, it's in October. The annual event teaches people about the wonder of migration as well as the need to protect migratory birds and their habitats.

WMBD is organized by Environment of the Americas, a nonprofit group that connects people with bird conservation through education and research. Every year the event has a new theme—2019 was Protect Birds: Be the Solution for Plastic Pollution. A new action for bird conservation was announced each day. The action for May 31, the day I was writing this, was "Learn a new bird song." Anyone can get involved. Join a WMBD celebration near you, and if you can't find one, organize one and invite your friends and neighbors to join you.

BIRD BRAINS AT WORK

Turned on by birds and citizen science? Maybe you're inspired to work in a bird-related field. Since the Greek philosopher Aristotle studied migration, scientists in many fields have focused their attention on birds. Ornithology, biology, ecology and geography are all examples of scientific fields in which a person can choose to study birds. But don't stop there. Bird studies have also contributed to the fields of navigation, aerodynamics, neurobiology and physiology. Wildlife rescue and rehabilitation, environmental education, nonprofit conservation work and even the arts— photography, painting or writing—are other areas in which you can put your love of and interest in birds to good use. Maybe you'll rescue an endangered species, discover a new bird or invent a 100 percent bird-safe way to make fossil-fuel-free energy.

ZOOS FOR CONSERVATION

The California condor, once a common scavenging bird in western North America, was almost wiped out by poaching, habitat loss, collisions with power lines, cyanide poisoning from traps set for coyotes, and lead poisoning from ammunition in their scavenged prey. By 1969 only 22 birds were left. The US government placed the condor on the endangered-species list. But the population continued to decrease. By 1985

TWEETS FROM THE FLYWAY

It was 4 a.m. My children and I were lying on hard ground in the middle of a damp Vancouver Island forest, in the dark and the cold, looking up though an opening in the trees. The sky started to lighten. We waited… and waited. Suddenly *whoosh!* A bird flew across the opening. *Whoosh!* There was another, and then we heard the calls of the birds: *kir, kir, kir.* Everyone gave a whispered cheer.

We were helping Dr. Alan Burger count marbled murrelets. The small, football-shaped seabirds live at sea except in the spring, when they fly inland to nest high in the moss-covered branches of huge old conifer trees. Lying on the ground waiting for murrelets is a typical task in the life of an ornithologist. Alan has devoted much of his working life to trying to figure out why marbled murrelet populations are declining, so that they can be better protected. He also spends time as an onboard naturalist on educational cruises to the Antarctic and the Arctic, teaching the passengers about the polar birds they see along the way. I'd say he has a wonderful job.

TWEETS FROM THE FLYWAY

Since 2012 enthusiastic Canadian and American volunteers and scientists have been working together to bring western bluebirds back to the Cowichan Valley in British Columbia. The beautiful blue-and-rusty-orange birds disappeared from the area in the 1990s, when much of their Garry oak meadow habitat was lost to roads, buildings and farms. The Bring Back the Bluebirds team has worked with scientists to transfer bluebirds from a healthy population in Washington State to British Columbia, a process called translocation. Team members install nest boxes to replace lost nesting habitat and walk established bluebird trails to monitor active nests. Volunteers raise mealworms to feed to the bluebirds. The bluebirds have started breeding, producing young and returning to the valley on their own. Every spring, colored bands are attached to the legs of all the new chicks, a technique called banding, which helps the project managers keep track of where the birds travel. By the spring of 2018, 42 western bluebird chicks had been born and banded. The bluebirds may always need assistance from humans in order to survive in the habitat that is left. But the project has kindled more public interest to protect the remaining endangered Garry oak meadows for all the plants and animals that rely on them.

Western bluebird and chick in the Cowichan Valley, BC. BARRY HETSCHKO

only nine birds remained. Drastic action was needed. All nine wild birds were captured, and a *conservation breeding* program started. It wasn't easy. Condors don't have chicks until they are six years old, and they lay only one egg a year. But the biologists patiently persisted. Today the population of condors has grown to about 400 birds. Over half of them have been released back into the wild and are flying free in California, Arizona and Mexico.

When you hear the word *zoo*, do you think of entertainment or science? Most modern zoos serve both purposes. But some people believe that the most important role of zoos should be to provide a home for those critically endangered species, like the California condor, whose populations have reached such low numbers that they would become extinct if left in the wild. British author and conservationist Gerald Durrell started the Jersey Zoo and the Durrell Wildlife Conservation Trust on the island of Jersey. The zoo is the first ever to focus exclusively on

TWEETS FROM THE FLYWAY

Bird conservation can be as exciting as a good adventure novel. Here's what my cousin Lance Woolaver Jr., a conservation biologist and director of Wildlife Preservation Canada, told me about rescuing the critically endangered Madagascar pochard from extinction: "Our crew from the Durrell Wildlife Conservation Trust and the Wildfowl & Wetlands Trust went up the worst roads I've ever traveled and collected eggs by canoe from three wild nests. We hatched them in a tent in an incubator run by a generator on the side of the lake and then drove them back down to a town where there was electricity.

We kept them in a makeshift tank in a rundown bathroom at a hotel. We successfully raised the ducklings, built a special facility for them and bred them in captivity. Now, after nine years of hard work by a lot of dedicated people, there's a captive-bred population that will soon be reintroduced to another lake that is being restored and managed by a local community in the northern part of Madagascar. This amazing conservation success story combined research, going out and rescuing birds, captive breeding and working with local communities to reintroduce birds back to the wild and ensure the species' survival."

This captive endangered echo parakeet, part of a conservation breeding program in Mauritius, made friends with conservation biologist Lance Woolaver's son, Glen. The parakeet's young are released into the wild as part of a larger recovery program. LANCE WOOLAVER JR.

endangered-species conservation. Its staff carefully breed endangered birds and other animals and raise their young in captivity, at the zoo or in partner locations around the world. The main goal is to build up populations in safety and eventually return the offspring to the animal's natural habitat, a process called *reintroduction*. Durrell believed that while zoos are important for educating people about wildlife and natural history, their most important role is to keep endangered animals from becoming extinct. He also believed that entertainment should never be the purpose of a zoo. What do you think?

Conservation breeding and reintroduction programs have successfully saved many bird species from certain extinction, including the Madagascar pochard (a duck endemic to Madagascar), the Mauritius kestrel, pink pigeon and echo parakeet on the island of Mauritius, the Hawaiian goose, the black stilt in New Zealand, the Puerto Rican parrot and the Bali starling.

BIRD FROM A MAGIC HAT

It's one thing to protect and conserve an endangered species, but what about bringing back a bird that's been extinct for over a hundred years? A project called Revive and Restore is attempting to do just that with the passenger pigeon. Passenger pigeons were once the most abundant bird in North America. They traveled in flocks so large they darkened the sky and took hours to pass by a single location. Overzealous hunting wiped them out in only a few short decades. The last passenger pigeon, a female named Martha, died in the Cincinnati Zoo in 1914.

Revive and Restore biologists propose to "*de-extinct*" the species by using *genetic engineering* on a closely related bird,

TWEETS FROM THE FLYWAY

Wild-animal rehabilitation centers rescue injured animals, treat them and release them back into the wild when they are well. In 2017 Wild Arc, a center on southern Vancouver Island, treated more than 3,000 animals. Many of the center's clients are birds, from tiny hummingbirds to songbirds to eagles. Look for a wildlife rescue center near you. You can support their work by volunteering or donating money or supplies for the care of injured birds.

the band-tailed pigeon. They hope to recreate, over time, a species identical to the passenger pigeon. Sound like a science-fiction movie? Some think it's far-fetched. Critics say that even if it worked, the hybrid pigeons would never be the real thing, that they might not survive in today's fragmented habitats and might even become an invasive species.

A SAFE PLACE

It's truly amazing that biologists like my cousin Lance bring endangered birds back from the brink of extinction. Or that passenger pigeons might fill the skies of North America again in the future. But if those rescued birds have no natural habitat where they can safely live their lives in nature and provide important ecosystem services, they'll just be specimens in a zoo or a lab. *Protected areas* are places that are set aside for nature. These include parks, nature reserves, wilderness areas and conservation

Banding the legs of baby birds, like this western bluebird chick, with a unique color-coded identification band helps ornithologists keep track of where the birds go after they leave the nest and throughout their life. BILL PENNELL

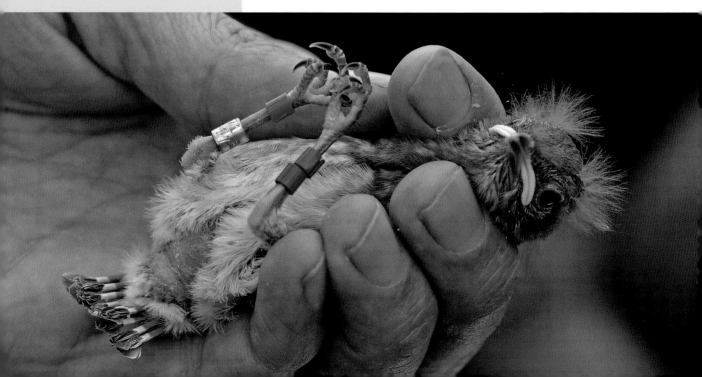

areas on both land and in the ocean. The best protected areas are those where no logging, mining, fishing or other harmful human activities are permitted. Where nature can be, well, natural. Where ecosystems can function with little or no interference from humans. Some protected areas are set aside for certain species of wildlife or to protect one or more ecosystems.

In 2010, 196 countries got together and created the Convention on Biological Diversity. The purpose of this international agreement is to stop the loss of biodiversity and ensure that the world's resources are used sustainably and fairly by all. One of the goals of the agreement is to protect at least 17 percent of the planet's land area and at least 10 percent of the ocean by 2020.

So how are we doing? The IUCN produces a *Protected Planet Report* every few years. According to the 2018 report almost 15 percent of the earth's land surface and inland waters and just over 7 percent of the global ocean were protected. Except for the ocean, we're getting close.

But don't celebrate yet. Protected areas work best if they represent all ecosystems, are interconnected and are fair to the people who live there. Some protected areas are better at safeguarding nature than others. Many ecosystems have much less area protected than others do. As of 2018, only 1 percent of the ocean area outside any country's control was protected. Some countries are doing a better job of protecting their land and water than others are. Some scientists believe the target goals are too low. Nature Needs Half is a science-based campaign to protect 50 percent of the planet's land and water by 2050—an ambitious goal, but the people involved believe it's possible. They're starting with the last large areas of

This red-winged blackbird lives in safety at the Tule Lake National Wildlife Refuge in California.
ROBERT MUTCH/SHUTTERSTOCK.COM

Visitors to the Currumbin Wildlife Sanctuary in Queensland, Australia, have fun feeding resident lorikeets. The sanctuary uses the income from tourist visits to support a wildlife hospital and many other wildlife-conservation projects in Australia. JACSON7788/DREAMSTIME.COM

wilderness: the northern boreal forest, the Amazon basin and Antarctica.

So how much area has been protected for birds? Any area that protects habitat will benefit the birds that live there. But a number of organizations are conserving habitat specifically for birds. The nonprofit organization BirdLife International has developed more than 12,000 Important Bird and Biodiversity Areas (IBAs) for the conservation of bird populations. Local conservation groups participating in BirdLife's Local Empowerment Program ensure that the IBAs in their area are conserved, managed and defended on behalf of the birds. In Canada, there are 325 IBA reserves with a total of 74 million acres (30 million hectares) designated for 520 bird species. There's one not far from my home. Have a look at the "Data Zone" on BirdLife's website to find an IBA near you.

FLYING LESSON

When I was young I often had dreams in which I could fly like a bird. I still close my eyes and imagine that feeling of exhilaration, weightlessness and freedom. Do you have flying dreams too? Wouldn't it be wonderful to soar high in the sky or across the ocean like a bird? People have been trying to find ways to fly since the time of the ancient Greeks. Artificial wings, sails and gliders have all been used in attempts to mimic bird flight, some more successfully than others.

I can't teach you to fly, but I hope this book has given you the next best thing—a desire to keep birds in flight. Every action you take to do that will make a difference. Whether you learn more about birds and appreciate them for their intrinsic value, make choices in your life that improve the lives of birds or flock together with bird

TWEETS FROM THE FLYWAY

Every summer near my home, I love hearing the beautiful spiraling call of the Swainson's thrush. In winter the thrush migrates south as far as Colombia, where I hope it finds safe haven in the El Dorado Reserve in the Sierra Nevada de Santa Marta mountain range. The endangered Santa Marta parakeet and 18 other endangered bird species, such as the Santa Marta screech-owl, also live in the reserve. The reserve was created in 2010 as a joint project of the American Bird Conservancy (ABC) and Colombia's Fundación ProAves. ABC has created more than 70 reserves for birds in 15 countries, covering a total of one million acres (4,046 square kilometers). The nonprofit aims to expand its reserve system so that all endangered bird species in the Americas have a safe place to live. Give ABC a cheer or a hand. It is already halfway there.

The endangered Santa Marta sabrewing is protected in the El Dorado Reserve, an Important Bird and Biodiversity Area.
JIRI REBICEK/SHUTTERSTOCK.COM

lovers of all ages, you'll be helping to keep common birds common and endangered birds from becoming extinct. Birds can't protect habitat, eliminate pesticides, get rid of invasive species or reduce greenhouse gases. They need people to do it for them. Be a bird ally. You'll be flying high in the eyes of birds and bird lovers everywhere.

YOUNG BIRDERS

Claire Wayner, a young birder from Baltimore, Maryland, started birding in 2012 as a member of the Youth Maryland Ornithological Society. In 2016 she co-founded Baltimore Beyond Plastic, a student group that spearheaded successful campaigns to ban Styrofoam, a single-use plastic that is deadly to birds and other wildlife. Claire currently attends Princeton University and co-leads the Princeton Birding Society, which sponsors regular bird walks to inspire her fellow students to appreciate birds and conservation. She plans to work in environmental and climate policy after graduation.

KOJO BAIDOO

GLOSSARY

adaptation—the process of change whereby an organism's physical or behavioral traits become better suited to its environment (see also *natural selection*)

binomial—in biology, a name made up of two terms, the genus and the species; for example, *Homo sapiens*

biodegradable—able to be broken down by living organisms such as bacteria into small, harmless parts

biodiversity—the variety of life found in a particular ecosystem

bioindicator—a species or ecological community that indicates the state or health of the environment in which it lives

bioturbation—the mixing up, or reworking, of soils and sediments by moving organisms such as worms

brood patch—a featherless patch that forms on the breast or abdomen of an adult bird to keep the egg or chicks warm against the adult's skin

call—a short sound made by a bird to communicate its location or warn other birds of a threat

citizen scientist—a volunteer like you and me who helps scientists collect information relating to the natural world

climate change—a change in global or regional climate patterns, attributed largely to increased levels of atmospheric carbon dioxide and other greenhouse gases, which are produced by the use of fossil fuels; see also *greenhouse gas*

conservation breeding—the process of breeding rare and endangered wild animals in a controlled environment such as a zoo or wildlife reserve with the goal of increasing their population and releasing them back into the wild; also known as captive breeding

de-extinct—to recreate an extinct species or one very similar to it using techniques such as cloning or selective breeding

ecological footprint—the impact of human activities as measured by the amount of the earth's resources it takes to produce the goods consumed, and the pollutants and waste their production creates

ecosystem—the network of plants, animals and other living microorganisms interacting with the nonliving environment as a functional unit

ecosystem conversion—the permanent conversion of a natural ecosystem, such as a forest, to an artificial human-made environment such as a road or a city

ecosystem services—the benefits to people of healthily functioning ecosystems, including provisioning (such as supplying food and water), regulating (such as controlling climate and disease), supporting (forming soil, producing oxygen and cycling nutrients) and cultural (recreational and spiritual contributions)

embryo—a vertebrate at any stage of development prior to birth or hatching

endemic—found only in a particular geographic area

evolution—the scientific theory explaining the appearance of new species and varieties through natural selection and other biological processes such as genetic mutation

extinction—the disappearance of a species from the earth

fair trade—the production and sale of products from developing countries whereby the producers receive a fair price, workers and farmers are treated ethically, and environmentally sustainable practices are promoted

food miles—the distance an item of food travels from its place of production to the consumer

food web—the interconnected network of predator-prey interactions within an ecological community (a food chain describes the order in which organisms rely on one another for food) frequency—the number of vibrations produced by a sound in one second

gene—the basic unit of DNA by which genetic information is passed from parent to offspring

genetic engineering—the science of changing the genes of a plant or animal to produce a desired result

genus—a biological ranking that includes one or more species of animals or plants that are closely related to one another

global warming—a gradual increase in the average temperature of the earth's atmosphere and the ocean, a change that is believed to be permanently altering the earth's climate

greenhouse gas—a gas in the atmosphere, such as carbon dioxide and methane, that absorbs and emits heat

incubation—maintenance of the conditions ideal to an embryo's development, such as a mother bird sitting on or otherwise protecting her eggs before they hatch

intrinsic value—the perceived value of an entity in and of itself, on the basis of its naturally occurring characteristics

invasive species—a non-native species, introduced accidentally or deliberately to an area, that becomes a problem to the native species or ecosystems

migratory—refers to a species that travels (migrates) between two different geographic regions to get what it needs to feed or breed

mismatch—a problem in timing whereby the right food supply or breeding conditions are not present at the time a migratory organism needs them, usually because of changes in climate

natural selection—the process whereby the individuals or groups that have adapted best to their environment survive and reproduce, passing along the successful traits to their offspring

neonicotinoids, or neonics—a class of insecticides with a chemical structure similar to nicotine that acts on the nervous system of insects

nutrients—substances needed by plants and animals in order to live and grow

ornithologist—a biologist who specializes in the scientific study of birds

pair-bonding—an exclusive union with a single mate for a period of time

pollination—the transfer of pollen from the male part of a plant to the female part of the same or another plant to form seeds

primary productivity—the rate at which organisms (mainly plants and algae) convert the sun's energy by photosynthesis into organic compounds; all life on earth relies on primary productivity

protected area—a location on land or in the ocean that is protected from development to conserve its natural, ecological or cultural values, such as a park, conservation area or nature reserve

raptor—a meat-eating bird such as a hawk, eagle, vulture or falcon that hunts for food or feeds on dead animals; also called a bird of prey

reintroduction—the return of a species to its former natural habitat

song—a series of musical sounds produced by a bird to attract a mate or defend a territory

sonogram—a visual representation of birdsong in the form of a graph; also called a spectrogram

species—a group of related organisms capable of interbreeding

syrinx—the branched vocal organ of birds; each of the two branches is controlled separately

taxonomy—the classification and naming of plants and animals according to their natural relationships and common history

wavelength—in relation to light, the distance between one crest (or trough) of a wave and the next; the wavelength of light determines its color; for example, the color red has a wavelength of 700 nanometers (a nanometer is one billionth of a meter)

zooplankton—tiny floating or weakly swimming animals in a body of water

RESOURCES

BOOKS

Calderwood, Damon, and Donald E. Waite. *Birding for Kids: A Guide to Finding, Identifying and Photographing Birds in Your Area*. Victoria, BC: Heritage House, 2020.

Thompson, Bill, III. *The Young Birder's Guide to Birds of North America*. Boston, MA: Houghton Mifflin Harcourt, 2012.

Brandt, DeAnna. *Bird Log Kids*. Cambridge, MN: Adventure Publications, 1998.

Harrison, George H. *Bird Watching for Kids: Bite-Sized Learning and Backyard Projects*. Minocqua, WI: Willow Creek Press, 2015.

WEBSITES

American Birding Association: aba.org

American Bird Conservancy: abcbirds.org

Audubon Society: audubon.org

Birdlife International (Nature's Hero Award, Spring Alive Project): birdlife.org

Bird Studies Canada programs: Doug Tarry Young Ornithologists, Christmas Bird Count for Kids, Project Bird Feeder, Partners in Flight, Schoolyard Bird Blitz, North American Bird Conservation Initiative: birdscanada.org

Conservation Youth Corp: cvc.ca/cyc

Cornell Lab of Ornithology's BirdSleuth, NestWatch and
Great Backyard Bird Count: birds.cornell.edu or
nestwatch.org

Durrell Wildlife Conservation Trust: durrell.org

Earth Rangers: earthrangers.com

eBird: ebird.org

eBird For Young Birders: ebird.org/about/resources/
for-young-birders

FLAP Canada (Fatal Light Awareness Program): flap.org
and birdsafe.ca

Flying Wild: flyingwild.org

Forest and Bird Youth NZ: forestandbird.org.nz/home

International Vulture Awareness Day: vultureday.org

Keep Animals Safe: keepanimalssafe.ca

Kiwi Guardians—Track Your Cat: doc.govt.
nz/parks-and-recreation/places-to-go/
toyota-kiwi-guardians

Nature Kids BC: naturekidsbc.ca

Oriental Bird Club Nepal: orientalbirdclub.org

Project Beak: projectbeak.org

Young Birders Program, BC Field Ornithologists:
www.bcfo.ca/bcfo-young-birder-program

UK Royal Society for the Protection of Birds
(Wildlife Explorers, Big Garden Bird Watch,
BirdTrack): rspb.org.uk

Wildfowl & Wetlands Trust: wwt.org.uk

Young Birders: youngbirders.aba.org

World Migratory Bird Day: migratorybirdday.org

ACKNOWLEDGMENTS

Bird's-Eye View was inspired by my volunteer work with the Thetis Island Nature Conservancy in my community. We've protected two large pieces of land as nature reserves to make sure the birds and other wildlife always have a safe place to live. We've put up nest boxes for owls and operate a nature house where people of all ages learn about the environment and how to be a good steward of the land and water. This book was also inspired by the birds that live in the forest and on the ocean near my home. I see birds every day. As I've learned more about them, I've realized how many of them are under threat from human activities.

I'm not an ornithologist. I don't know the name of every bird I see or hear. I don't have a Life List. But I wanted to use my skills as a writer and a biologist to help young people learn about birds and bird conservation so that there are more of us on the planet working to help protect birds at risk and to keep common birds common. So I had to do lots of research. I read many books about birds. Here are a few I found very interesting and helpful: *Silence of the Songbirds*, by Bridget Stutchbury; *Why Birds Matter*, edited by Çağan H. Şekercioğlu, Daniel G. Wenny and Christopher J. Whelan; *Birds and Climate Change*, by James W. Pearce-Higgins and Rhys E. Green; and *The Genius of Birds*, by Jennifer Ackerman. I gathered information from the websites of amazing bird-related organizations, including the Cornell Lab of Ornithology, the American Birding Association, the American Bird Conservancy, the Audubon Society and BirdLife International. The story of Gabi came from a 2015 BBC News Magazine article by journalist Katy Sewall. Most important, I gave my manuscript to people knowledgeable about birds to read. I'm grateful to Alan Burger, Lance Woolaver Jr., Rina Nichols and Bridget Stutchbury for their invaluable comments. Any errors are my own. Thank you also to Tory Stevens and Gary Geddes for their feedback and to my agent, John Pearce, for his unwavering support and encouragement.

Last but not least, the folks at Orca Book Publishers embraced *Bird's-Eye View* with enthusiasm and produced it wonderfully with their truly amazing expertise. Sarah Harvey, Ruth Linka and Andrew Wooldridge deserve a special shout-out for their dedication to publishing educational and inspiring children's books that make the world a better place. Thank you all!

INDEX

*Page numbers in **bold** indicate an image caption.*

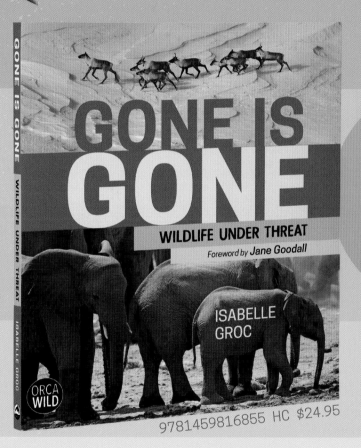

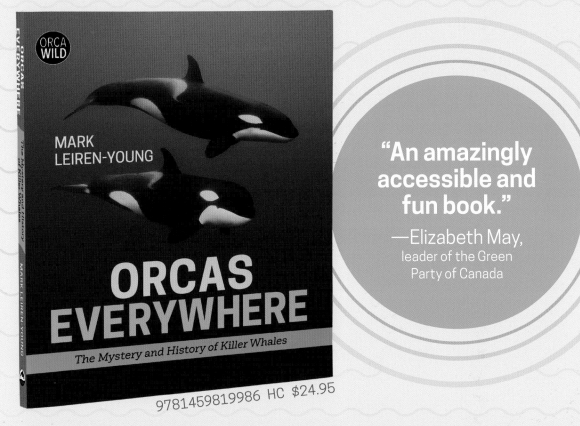